*An Outline of Modern Russian
Literature*
(1880-1940)

AN OUTLINE OF MODERN RUSSIAN LITERATURE

(1880-1940)

By

ERNEST J. SIMMONS

GREENWOOD PRESS, PUBLISHERS
WESTPORT, CONNECTICUT

Copyright 1943 by Cornell University

Originally published in 1944 by Cornell Unviersity Press, Ithaca, New York

Reprinted with the permission
of Cornell University Press

First Greenwood Reprinting 1971

Library of Congress Catalogue Card Number 75-138599

SBN 8371-5801-X

Printed in the United States of America

Preface

THE purpose of this little book is to provide a brief guide to the principal writers and works of modern Russian literature for those who do not know Russian. It is unnecessary any longer to apologize for an ignorance of recent Russian literature because of an ignorance of the language. Although translations of recent Russian poetry are by no means abundant, there is now a very considerable body of translated fiction and drama. Translations of the chief productions of most of the authors treated in this book will be found in the bibliography of translations at the end. As a further aid to readers who lack a knowledge of the language, all Russian names are accented.

For several helpful suggestions, I am indebted to Mr. Peter Pertzoff, instructor in Russian at Cornell University, and for bibliographical assistance to Mr. Eric T. Schuler and Patricia Beesley.

E. J. S.

Contents

	PAGE
PREFACE	v
I. A BACKWARD GLANCE	3
II. THE NOVEL (1880–1900)	7
III. POETRY (1880–1900)	12
IV. PROSE FICTION AFTER CHÉKHOV (1900–1910)	14
V. THE MODERNIST MOVEMENTS OF THE 1890's	23
VI. THE SYMBOLIST MOVEMENT	27
VII. THE REVOLUTION OF 1917	36
VIII. THE BEGINNINGS OF SOVIET FICTION	42
IX. FICTION DURING THE FIRST FIVE-YEAR PLAN	49
X. SOVIET POETRY	58
XI. SOVIET DRAMA	65
XII. RECENT TRENDS IN SOVIET LITERATURE	69
BIBLIOGRAPHY: A SELECTIVE GUIDE TO MODERN RUSSIAN LITERATURE IN ENGLISH TRANSLATION (1880–1940)	75
INDEX	91

*An Outline of Modern Russian
Literature
(1880-1940)*

CHAPTER I

A Backward Glance

RUSSIAN literature, like some ubiquitous character in an Elizabethan drama, is always being "discovered" by foreign critics and always to no purpose. A few great names, such as Dostoyévsky, Turgénev, and Tolstóy, are well known in Western Europe and America, but they seem to exist as isolated phenomena in a literary void. Their place in the orderly progression of Russian literary history, and their relations to the bone and gristle of movements and to predecessors and followers are hardly ever considered.

Yet the pattern of Russia's literary development is extremely illuminating, both with reference to the growth of the country's culture and the contributions to it of individual poets, novelists, and critics. In a way unexampled in Western European countries, Russian literature reflected the ebb and flow of political and social thought, for from 1825 a constant struggle against the government, either openly or underground, occupied the minds of most thinking people. The government itself took an unwholesome proprietary interest in what authors wrote, but only since the Soviet Revolution, when the secret archives of the old régime were thrown open, has it become possible to estimate fully the effects on literature of censorship and other means of official repression.

Not infrequently an exaggerated emphasis has been placed upon the so-called "tendentious" nature of Russian literature. Its tendentiousness existed more in the minds and demands of professional native critics than in the actual performance of great imaginative writers. From the time of V. G. Belínski (1810–1848), the father of Russian literary criticism, critics among the radical intelligentsia, usually the most able and popular, tended to approve all literary productions on the basis of their political and social significance. Aesthetic matters of form and expression were accorded a secondary place or no place at all in the prevailing criticism. The liberal reforms of the reign of Alexander II (1855–1881) encouraged the hopes of progressive thinkers for still more radical changes in the political and social scheme of things, and critics increased their demands that literature should serve a utilitarian purpose and reflect the burning questions of the day. To a considerable extent literature did just this, but it is a striking fact that the famous novelists in the richest period of Russian fiction kept singularly aloof from tendentious themes. Goncharóv, Dostoyévsky, Turgénev, Tolstóy, and Leskóv for the most part plowed their own furrows of art without turning to the left or to the right in order to satisfy the social demands of the critics. Such distinguished novels as *Oblómov, A Nest of Gentlefolk, War and Peace, Anna Karénina* and *The Brothers Karamázov* are unusually free from tendentiousness. Their authors in each case had a personal message to preach, but they did not allow it to obtrude upon the artistic unity of their efforts, nor could their works be labeled novels of purpose or social novels.

The violent death of Alexander II at the hands of revolutionary terrorists in 1881 came at the end of Russia's greatest age of fiction, for with very few exceptions the best work of the foremost novelists had already been done. Dostoyévsky died in 1881 and Turgénev two years later. Tolstóy lived on to 1910, but in 1880, after he had experienced his unique spiritual transformation, he turned his back on the kind of art that had produced *War and Peace* and *Anna Karénina*. He did not break with art entirely, as is commonly asserted, for among his extensive works after 1880 are such significant productions as *The Power of Darkness, The Kreutzer Sonata,* and *Resurrection*. But he did endeavor to make his art serve the new spiritual and moral values by which he tried to live.

In still another important respect the assassination of Alexander II marked the end of an old and the beginning of a new literary era. For the murder of the tsar provoked a period of black reaction, comparable to that of Nicholas I's reign after the failure of the Decembrist Revolt of 1825. The revolutionary movement was suppressed, radical publications were banned, and in general progressive intellectual thinking dwindled to a vanishing point. The country foundered in reaction, and the best minds surrendered to utter boredom or impotent aspirations.

In such circumstances it was only natural that during the reign of Alexander III (1881–1894) literature should react violently against the utilitarian direction and social significance of the preceding period. For the most part authors eschewed the tendentious and preferred to grapple with a content of more universal implications. The new criticism no longer cried out for literature with a social purpose that would satisfy the hopes of the public for change; rather it dwelt upon the eternal questions of art and called for more attention to form and to beauty of expression. As an indication of the new tastes, even poetry, which had been relatively dormant in the previous great age of prose, was revived. In place of the contentious and polemical attitude in literature came one of timidity and frustration, for it was a timid and frustrated time in Russian national life.

CHAPTER II

The Novel (1880-1900)

THE towering shadow of the white-bearded prophet Tolstóy dominated the fiction writers from 1880 to 1900. It was the great novels before his spiritual revelation that they sought to imitate and not the occasional but fine tales that amid a sea of religious and didactic works seemed to drop from his pen by chance after 1880. Nor did the younger writers grasp the art of his new prose style, at its best a beautifully chastened medium of expression that placed no obstacle between author and reader.

One of the first and best of the new generation of fiction writers influenced by Tolstóy, and partly by Turgénev, was V. M. Gárshin (1855–1888). The fame of his tragically brief creative life rests on his collected short stories, the most notable of which, particularly *The Red Flower* (1883), reveal a moral sensitivity and an infinite compassion for the injured and thwarted victims of man's inhumanity. The matter and not the manner of his narratives pleases, and his fondness for the morbid became the hallmark of so many of the writers of this feckless age.

Of a group of minor novelists, the only one whose contemporary popularity seems to have left any memorable trace today is A. I. Értel (1855–1908): his two-volume novel *The Gardénins* (1898) still makes good reading. It is an extensive family novel of life on a huge estate in South Central Russia. Tolstóy especially praised it for its homely, realistic dialogue, and in this respect, as well as in the characterizations of local types and in the poetical description of nature, the work has a large increment of the master's art.

With the literary voice of political and social criticism effectively muzzled in Russia during this period, it remained for émigré writers to carry on abroad a practice that already amounted to a tradition of vigorous and often brilliant writing. But there was no one among the exiled authors then who could compare with such a distinguished figure as Hérzen in the previous generation. Unquestionably the best of them was Peter Kropótkin (1842–1921), a leading theorist of revolutionary anarchism, who early in his career was forced to flee abroad. Among the numerous productions of his long life, perhaps the only one to win an enduring place as literature is *Memoirs of a Revolutionary* (1899), originally written in English. It is a work of first-rate importance in the development of Russian revolutionary thought, but it is also skillfully written and of considerable literary worth.

If radicalism may be said to have had a real literary representative during this period of repression, it was V. G. Korolénko (1853–1921). Membership in a secret political organization resulted in his exile to Siberia in 1879, but his experiences there did nothing to sour his warm love of humanity and they provided a storehouse

THE NOVEL (1880-1900)

of material for his fiction. Thus his first important work, *Makár's Dream* (1885), written in the year he was allowed to return to Russia proper, is the story of a native Yakut. Succeeding tales draw upon his life in Siberia. With a poet's feeling, and directly in the tradition of Turgénev, he describes the stark beauty of the snowy wastes of the north. These poetic descriptions provide atmosphere for characters who are often victims of man's exploitation. At best, however, Korolénko's radicalism is a form of idealism, a yearning after that state of society when man's innate goodness will finally triumph over evil. Invariably he brings his stories down to earth by a delightful humor, which in its pure form, as in *The Day of Atonement*, is as charming as Gógol's fun-making in his early tales. His last considerable work, *The History of My Contemporary* (1909), is really an autobiography. It lacks the poetic feeling of his tales, but is filled with the two characteristic traits of his art—humor and human sympathy. Korolénko deserves a place as a minor classic among Russian writers.

Indeed, Korolénko's rank as a writer of fiction would have been first among his contemporaries if his principal rival had not been Antón Pávlovich Chékhov (1860-1904). Son of a former serf and trained in medicine, Chékhov early began to support himself by writing humorous sketches for the newspapers. When these stories were collected in book form in 1886, they met with immediate success with the public, although critics slighted the work. Few of these early tales have been translated into English. Written for cheap comic newspapers, they are little removed from buffoonery and vulgarity, and often instead of a note of human sympathy they contain an undisguised sneer at man's weakness.

Released from his drudgery to the comic newspapers by improved financial circumstances after 1886, Chékhov began to write stories that contained his characteristic elements of content, humor, style, and atmosphere for which he later became famous. It was not until *A Dreary Story* in 1889, however, that Chékhov entered upon his mature period. Here we find that mutual lack of understanding among characters and the psychological development of a mood that combine to form the "Chekhovian state of mind" so familiar in his best known tales. In this new manner there soon followed those perfect little masterpieces, *The Duel, Ward 6, An Anonymous Story, My Life, Peasants, The Lady with the Dog, At Christmas Time,* and *In the Ravine.* These stories are tight, compact expressions of autumnal moods, in which subtly contrived emotional and symbolic overtones harmonize with a marvelously unified construction. His characters lack individuality, for the emphasis is placed on the creation of a poetic mood rather than on the differentiation of human personality.

This same trait is also very pronounced in his highly popular and unique dramas. He had begun to write plays as early as 1885, but with indifferent success. It was with *The Seagull* in 1896, followed by *Uncle Ványa* (1896), *The Three Sisters* (1900), and *The Cherry Orchard* (1903), that he achieved renown in the history of Russian drama. The striking undramatic quality of his plays is not an innovation, as is commonly supposed, but simply a further refinement of a characteristic to be found in certain of the plays of Ostróvski and especially in those of Turgénev. In other respects Chékhov's plays are unique in that they avoid subject-matter, plot, and action, and strive to create a poetic atmosphere. The theme of the play is a mood, and the characters display that mutual unintelligibility so pronounced in his fiction. Again as in the stories, the dominant note is one of gloom, depression, and futility subtly intensified by an underlying emotional symbolism.

CHAPTER III

Poetry (1880-1900)

AFTER the Golden Age of Poetry with Púshkin and his immediate disciples (1800-1840), the muse was silenced, or nearly so, by the wonderful flowering of prose fiction. Only the lyric beauty and exquisite craftsmanship of Tyútchev and Fet, and the social realism of the vigorous verse of Nekrásov could compete for public favor with the great novels of Goncharóv, Dostoyévsky, Turgénev, and Tolstóy. In the late 1880's and early 1890's, however, there was something of a revival in poetry. "Beauty" and "melancholy" became popular themes. The so-called "civic poets" mouthed their melancholy over social injustice in indifferent verse, and the "art-for-art's sake poets" indulged a love for pure beauty which they distilled from a variety of lost causes.

The most popular of the civic poets was Semyón Nádson (1862-1887). His brief creative life was dedicated to themes of reform, but he lacked faith in his own ideals and the spiritual and imaginative power to clothe them in language of transcending beauty. Nádson's extensive contemporary success must be attributed to his smooth, effortless verse that was highly quotable and echoed the

POETRY (1880-1900)

underlying sense of futility so persistent at that time. His principal rival for popular favor was A. N. Apúkhtin (1841-1893), whose poetry reflected the same impotent regret, but it was a hedonist's regret for the lost pleasures of youth and was expressed in a more virile, realistic verse. Rising considerably above the thriving but undistinguished level of poetry during this period was the verse of V. S. Solovyóv (1853-1900). A man of extraordinary contrasts in his intellectual life, Solovyóv has won the reputation of being one of Russia's most brilliant philosophical thinkers and cleverest writers of nonsense verse. In poetry he combined the verbal wit and fun-making of a Thomas Hood with the profound mystical experiences of a Blake. A mystical love affair with the Finnish Lake Saima, for example, resulted, in the 1890's, in a series of beautiful lyrics, often difficult to comprehend without an intimate knowledge of the poet's religious and philosophical thought. His longest poem, *Three Meetings,* reveals a characteristic thinness of form, but it also combines in a paradoxical manner humorous irreverence with a mystical meaning at once sublime and baffling.

CHAPTER IV

Prose Fiction After Chékhov (*1900-1910*)

BENEATH the oppression and sense of frustration in the 1880's and 1890's, revolutionary forces were slowly but surely gathering. Driven underground by the vigilance of the tsar's secret police, this radical movement could find no legal expression in literature. A new force had also entered the prolonged struggle against autocracy —that of Russian Marxism. Lénin hímself was one of the original Marxists of the 1890's. The fundamentally scientific doctrine of Marx appealed strongly to disillusioned intellectuals and brought new hope to the whole radical movement. Further, the Marxists looked for support not to the peasantry, as had the Populists, but to the growing proletarian class whose numbers had been tremendously increased by the swift growth of Russian capitalism over this period. By one of those miracles of compromise, all liberal and radical forces managed to form a united front against the government in a widespread demand for reform. Their efforts culminated in the disastrous 1905 Revolution. Although certain gains were made, such as the establishment of the Duma, the high hopes of the revolutionists were blasted. Profound disillusionment with

PROSE FICTION AFTER CHÉKHOV (1900–1910)

the whole radical movement set in, and their feelings found literary expression in an anti-political individualism, in the growth of aestheticism, and often in fiction of a pronounced erotic nature. The most popular school of fiction at this time, and one that drew much of its inspiration from the realism of Chékhov, had as its earliest and most powerful representative Maxím Górky (pseud. of A. M. Péshkov, 1869–1939). Górky's initial and perhaps most significant service was to liberate Russian realism from its conservative traditions. For the realism of the great novelists from 1850 to 1900 had been subject to the same restraints and conventions as the realism of English Victorian fiction. Górky belonged to the provincial proletariat, and he already had had a background of bitter experiences among the lost men and women of Russia's lower depths, when he attracted international notice before he was thirty with two volumes of collected stories (1898). The realism of these early tales, such as *Makár Chúdra*, *Chelkásh*, and *Málva*, is combined with an infectious but blatant romanticism. The bracing, carefree atmosphere of the tales came as a welcome relief to readers who had grown weary of the gloom of Chékhov. Towards the end of his early period this youthful romanticism faded and realism became dominant. In *Twenty-Six Men and a Girl*, perhaps his finest short story, the realism is stark and cruel but faithful to experience, and the tale strikes a characteristic note —Górky's profound interest in the misery of Russia's masses; he does not condemn their misery in a didactic manner but reveals it in all its ugliness. In these forgotten people, however, he sees a poetry, a dignity and beauty, and a strength that will one day enable them to throw off their shackles.

To Górky's second period belong largely novels and dramas. The principal novels are *Fomá Gordéyev* (1899), *Three of Them* (1900–1901), *Mother* (1907), *A Confession* (1908), *Okúrov City* (1910), and *Matvéi Kozhemyákin* (1911). Nearly all of them are concerned with the vicious life and immorality of provincial Russia. Their sombre, bitter realism is relieved only by occasional figures who in their efforts to grasp the meaning of life strive for something better. Endless talk about the "meaning of life," a penchant for philosophizing that Górky never rid himself of, is one of the worst features of these novels. This same fault serves to make his plays (among the better known are *Petty Bourgeois*, 1901; *The Lower Depths*, 1902; *Suburbans*, 1904; *Children of the Sun*, 1905; *The Barbarians*, 1906; *Enemies*, 1907; *Vássa Zheleznóva*, 1911) rather bad imitations of Chékhov, although *The Lower Depths* achieved vast popularity both in and outside of Russia.

This period of novels and plays was soon followed by another, in which Górky devoted himself largely to autobiographical writing (*Childhood*, 1913; *Among Strangers*, 1915; *My Universities*, 1923), and to a wonderful volume of recollections of the authors he had known, such as Tolstóy, Korolénko, Chékhov, and Andréyev. These works are among his best, for they provided full scope for his unusual powers of realistic characterization and at the same time discouraged his fondness for prolix subjective philosophizing about life.

PROSE FICTION AFTER CHÉKHOV (1900-1910)

Górky's radical activities before 1917 and his declared sympathies for the communists won him a place as the foremost literary figure of the Soviet Revolution, a place that he retained until his death in 1939. He performed many valuable cultural services for the new régime, and scores of young Soviet authors regarded him reverently as their master. In 1924 appeared his *Notes from a Diary*, a striking collection of character studies, and this was followed by a series of novels, *Artamónov's Business* (1925; translated into English as *Decadence*), and *The Life of Klim Sámgin* (1928), composed of four volumes that bear the titles *Bystander, The Magnet, Other Fires,* and *The Spectre*. In this last effort, his *magnum opus*, Górky attempts to present the history of Russian life between 1880 and 1917. He is largely concerned with showing the gradual disintegration of the middle class before the impact of the social and economic conditions that led up to the Soviet Revolution. Although most of his fiction presents a picture of Russian life that is dark, cruel, and ugly, it is not essentially a pessimistic picture, for rising above the pervading gloom is always the vision of another brighter and happier Russia. That is, despite the unvarying fare of misery and oppression in his fiction, Górky always leaves you with the feeling that Russia is still the most wonderful country in the world, where "even the fools are original."

Around Górky and his publishing firm *Znánie,* there rallied a group of writers who reveled in outspoken realism and went as far in the direction of revolutionary protest as the government authorities would permit. The most prominent among them were E. N. Chírikov (1864–1932), V. V. Veresáyev (pseud. of V. V. Smidówicz, 1867–), Ivan Shmelyóv (1875–), A. S. Serafimóvich (pseud. of A. S. Popóv, 1863–), and Skitálets (pseud. of S. G. Petróv, 1868–1934). Most of their works have been forgotten, but Veresáyev and Serafimóvich have won a new popularity in the Soviet régime through novels distinctly sympathetic to the ideals of the Revolution. Veresáyev's *The Deadlock* (1922) depicts the civil war as experienced by the intelligentsia, and his *Sisters* (1933) contrasts the reactions of two sisters of utterly different temperaments to the new Socialist Russia. Serafimóvich's *The Iron Torrent* (1924), which described the civil war in the south of Russia, was regarded upon its appearance as the most Marxian work of fiction written since the Revolution. Of greater stature, however, were three or four authors who belonged to Górky's generation and in certain respects were influenced by him; but they were all men of original ability, and at least two of them possessed literary talent of a very high order.

The Duel (1905) made A. I. Kúprin (1870–1938) famous overnight. This novel of army life was the logical successor of a series of early stories, in which morbid young army officers brood over the meaning of life, and wretched soldiers suffer under the brutality of their superiors. There is more of the influence of Chékhov than Górky in it, and the character drawing is well done. Kúprin's succeeding novels, such as *Izumrúd, Sulamith* (1908), and *Yáma* (1910), were also quite popular, but they represent a falling-off in artistic power. Something of a sensation seeker

PROSE FICTION AFTER CHÉKHOV (1900-1910)

in subject-matter, his considerable talents were often forced to serve themes for which he had no natural aptitude. The works of Kipling and Jack London strongly attracted him, and, unlike most Russian writers of fiction, he possessed an unusual affinity for the Western story of heroic action. Several of his later tales in this vein, such as *Lieutenant-Captain Rýbnikov* (1906) and *The Bracelet of Garnets* (1911), were eminently successful and striking in their Górky-like handling of realistic details. At first opposed to the Soviet régime, Kúprin left the country and spent some years in France, but he later returned to the Soviet Union, where he died in 1938.

I. A. Búnin (1870-), although a nominal follower of Górky in his youth, has closer literary ties with such predecessors as Turgénev, Tolstóy, and Chékhov, and in some respects he is a finer artist than any of the writers of Górky's generation. He first attracted notice by a book of verse in 1891, and succeeding volumes won him a considerable reputation as a poet. A traditionalist in poetry, he has nothing refreshingly new to offer, unless it be exotic descriptions of nature. His approach is objective, his themes mostly impressions of nature, and his technique is entirely adequate though rarely very original.

Búnin's poetic gifts penetrate his prose style in both language and imagery, and it is as a novelist that he has achieved his greatest fame. His stories began to appear as early as 1892, but his first novel, *The Village*, was not published until 1909. This book was followed by some of his best fiction—*Sukhodól* (1911), *Ioánn the Weeper* (1913), *The Cup of Life* (1913), and his famous story *The*

19

Gentleman from San Francisco (1915). In 1918 Búnin left Soviet Russia and eventually settled in Paris. As an émigré, his work at first betrayed a diminution in power, especially in the tales in *The Rose of Jericho* (1924), but later pieces, such as *Mítya's Love* (1925), the age-old love tragedy of a disappointed youth, and *Arsényev's Life* (1927), a fine example of transposed biography, reveal Búnin at his best.

In *The Village* Búnin left behind him the sentimental stories of his early period and wrote a bitter realistic social novel of the misery and primitivism of Russian country life. The peasant is faithfully portrayed without any attempt at idealizing him. Búnin's early fault of excessive philosophizing is overcome in *Sukhodól*, perhaps his greatest work—the concentrated story of the disintegration of a landowning family told from the point of view of a female servant. Búnin is a strange combination of the realist and the romantic, and at his best he is one of the most original writers of Russian prose today.

The author who for a time became a serious rival of Górky for popular favor was Leoníd Andréyev (1871–1919). There is little to justify the belief that Andréyev was one of the first Russian symbolists. Among his earliest short stories, such as *Once Upon a Time There Lived* (1901) and *In the Fog* (1902), he showed himself a devotee of the new realism of Górky, and in his favorite themes of death and sex, a follower of Tolstóy—the Tolstóy of *The Death of Iván Ilyích* and *The Kreutzer Sonata*. After the failure of the 1905 Revolution, Andréyev catered to the widespread disillusion by treating the themes of death and sex in a morbid and sensational manner. He became the

PROSE FICTION AFTER CHEKHOV (1900-1910)

leader of a short-lived group of fiction writers whose outlook on life was entirely pessimistic and nihilistic. Andréyev's early style, which he had learned from Tolstóy's problem stories, is a restrained, logical, and effective style; but his later, sensational style is shrill, rhetorical, and full of bad taste. Yet this style was tremendously admired in his day as he used it in such famous stories as *The Red Laugh* (1904), *And So Is Was* (1906), *Judas Iscariot* (1907), and *The Curse of the Beast* (1908). Andréyev became a specialist in madness and horror, and his persistent message was physical death and the annihilation of society, morals, and culture. Occasionally he would revert to his early restraint, as in two of his finest tales, *The Governor* (1906) and *The Seven That Were Hanged* (1908), the latter a story of five terrorists and two common murderers who were sentenced to death. His plays, the best known of which are *The Life of Man* (1906) and *He Who Gets Slapped* (1914), are written in the tradition of Chékhov and Górky. Their rhetorical language, abstractions for characters, and infinite philosophizing were much praised in the author's day, but they make difficult reading now. Although highly representative of one phase of the period in which he lived, Andréyev by no means measured up to the qualities of the best artist. There was more virtuosity than enduring artistry in what he did, more tinsel and fake than sincerity and human sympathy. A few, very few of his tales, deserve a place in any anthology of Russian short stories; the rest time has already annihilated.

In this fiction of pessimism, the only popular rival of Andréyev was M. P. Artsybáshev (1878-1927). His enormously successful novel *Sánin* (1907) was a response to the sexual emancipation that reflected one aspect of the nihilism of despair that gripped the intelligentsia after the failure of the 1905 Revolution. The theme of the novel was one that has been run into the ground in modern fiction—be true to yourself and follow your natural inclinations. With Artsybáshev, the natural inclinations were all reduced to carnal desire for the other sex. There was no escape from sex, but the author's attempt to prove his thesis philosophically and psychologically is amateurish in the extreme. And with equally boring didacticism, Artsybáshev's second novel, *At the Brink* (1911–1912), revels in that other constant theme of Andréyev—death. While the public was in a mood for sex and death, Artsybáshev remained popular.

CHAPTER V

The Modernist Movements of the 1890's

VARIOUS forces were at work in the 1890's in opposition to the Górky-Andréyev school, and particularly to the dominance of social significance and nihilistic thought in literature. There was a definite turning away from civic morality to aestheticism, from duty to beauty, and cultural and individual values were stressed at the expense of political and social values. Most of the participators in this movement were brilliant intellectuals, and their efforts represented a lofty degree of cultural refinement that had never been achieved by any literary group in Russia hitherto. Aesthetic, mystic, and religious philosophers took part in this revolt against the civic-minded intelligentsia, and much of the impetus was provided by those extraordinary painters and writers on art, Diághilev and Benois, in their lavish monthly magazine, *Mir Iskússtva* (*The World of Art*), founded in 1898.

One of the earliest and most influential of the modernists was D. S. Merezhkóvski (1865–1941). After an initial volume of conventional verse in 1888, he emerged as the champion of the "new ideas" of a group of writers, among whom were prominently his talented wife, Zinaída Híppius (1869–), Mínski (pseud. of N. M. Vilénkin, 1855–1937), and Volýnski (pseud. of A. L. Flékser, 1863–1926). A certain vagueness characterized the revolt in its early stages, but over the next few years Merezhkóvski devoted a stream of philosophic criticism, historical novels, plays, and pamphlets to elaborating his central idea concerning the opposition of the Greek conception of the sanctity of the flesh and the Christian conception of the sanctity of the spirit and the necessity of uniting them in one synthesis. This antithetical approach in one aspect or another dominated nearly everything he wrote until it resulted in a kind of ideological madness that seriously vitiated his literary performance. Thus, in one of his best known works, *Tolstóy and Dostoyévsky* (1901–1902), Tolstóy becomes the "seer of the flesh" and Dostoyévsky the "seer of the spirit." This same antithetic tendency runs through his trilogy of historical novels, *Julian the Apostate; or, The Death of the Gods* (1896), *Leonardo da Vinci; or, The Gods Reborn* (1902), and *Peter and Alexis* (1905). Merezhkóvski's considerable literary talents were sacrificed to his passion for playing the philosopher and prophet. As the need to preach intensified itself, the content of his works grew more didactic and his style more shrill and unattractive. He was the founder of the Religious Philosophic Society which provided, toward the end of the last century, a meeting ground for God-seeking intellectuals. Opposed to the radicals at first, he eventually turned towards them in the hope of imbuing the movement with a religious faith. The Revolution of 1917 was a bitter disappointment to him, and he became one of its fiercest critics among the Russian émigrés. Most of Merezhkóvski's philosophical and religious thought is derivative, and his purely imaginative writing displays more scholarly erudition than creative power. The religious-philosophical speculation that possessed Merezhkóvski became the province of some of the most original minds at the end of the 1890's and the beginning of the twentieth century. As in the case of Merezhkóvski, Dostoyévsky inspired much of this theorizing. V. V. Rózanov (1856–1919) first attracted general attention by his study, *The Legend of the Grand Inquisitor* (1890), a penetrating commentary on this incident in *The Brothers Karamázov*. In a series of later works he went on to attack the ascetic religion of Christ to which he opposed the primitive naturalistic religion that he found in the Old Testament. Although profoundly mystical and religious, Rózanov preferred a faith more "natural" than orthodox Christianity. There is a pronounced immoralism in his thinking that takes the form of a phallic symbolism in the development of his religious philosophy. Most of his religious thought found expression in a series of books, the best known of which are *In the Realm of Riddle and Mystery* (1901), *The Russian Church* (1906), *The Dark Face* (1911), and *Moonlight Men* (1913).

Although a conservative in politics, Rózanov was strangely attracted by the youthful radical spirit that helped to bring about the 1905 Revolution, but it was more the detached interest of an acute philosophical mind in the psychology behind revolutionary action. His enthusiasm did not outlast the 1917 Revolution, which left him troubled in spirit and much embittered. Meanwhile he had produced one of his finest and most characteristic works, *Solitary Thoughts* (1912), a book of sayings and brief essays, remarkable for their originality in both form and content. With good effect he mined the same rich vein in *Fallen Leaves* (1913) and in *Fallen Leaves, a Second Basketful* (1915). Like Dostoyévsky, he possessed an uncanny intuitive insight into the riddle of human personality, and what touched him most deeply there—again like Dostoyévsky—was man's natural goodness.

Like Rózanov, Leo Shestóv (pseud. of L. I. Schwarzmann, 1866–1938), also an irrationalist and an immoralist, found his starting-point in Dostoyévsky, but he was also much influenced by Nietzsche, who attracted many Russian writers at this time. Shestóv warred against idealism in all its forms (*The Philosophy of Tragedy*, 1901, and *Potestas Clavium*, 1916). He was a seeker after God, but it was a God divorced from reason and the good, a God that transcended the traditional standards of morality and logic. Besides being highly independent thinkers, Rózanov and Shestóv are remarkable for the excellence of their prose style. Rózanov's style is extremely unorthodox in its use of various typographical devices to emphasize meaning, but it is rich in emotional shades and connotations and filled with intonations impossible to convey in translation. Shestóv's prose is a striking contrast to that of Rózanov; it is quintessentially classical, notable for its concentration, restraint, and balance.

CHAPTER VI

The Symbolist Movement

THE emphasis upon aesthetics and mysticism in the works of such writers as Merezhkóvski, Rózanov, and Shestóv provided an easy transition to symbolism, for a mystical interpretation of the world was an aesthetic principle held in common by nearly all the Russian symbolists from 1890 to 1910. Baudelaire and Mallarmé helped to inspire this new movement, but Russian writers, unlike the French, made a philosophy of symbolism as well as a new form of poetical expression. In a sense, Poe was a deeper influence than the French writers, and Dostoyévsky's strident individualism and tragic conception of life were at the very core of the evolution. A new vocabulary, or better, a new way of using old phrases, a subordination of sense to sound, and a symbolic use of words produced that impression of obscurity which became associated with the writers of the movement. They envisaged the world as a system of symbols, and everything became significant to them, not by itself alone, but as a reflection of something else.

Perhaps to Valéri Bryúsov (1873–1924) belongs the credit for starting the movement with a collection of poems published in *The Russian Symbolists* in 1894. For some ten years he was regarded as a kind of poetical fraud, and his verses were the chief butt of the critics, but by 1906 he had won his long battle for recognition and was regarded as the head of a school that literally represented the whole of Russian poetry at the time. His poem *Stephanos*, published in 1905, aroused enthusiasm, and his review, *The Scales*, was accepted as the most cultured and authoritative publication in the country. Though a weaver of gorgeous imagery that is often more gaudy than meaningful, Bryúsov's poetic and even his prose style (his best prose tales are *The Republic of the Southern Cross, On the Altar of Victories*, and *The Fire Angel*, 1907–1908) bears often the traces of chilly, studious premeditation.

K. D. Balmónt (1867–1943) shared with Bryúsov the honor of being one of the first of the symbolists in the field by virtue of his early volume of verse, *Under Northern Skies* (1894). There is more sound than sense in Balmónt's poetry, which has nothing of the intellectual quality of Bryúsov's and very little of the symbolic quality characteristic of the whole school. Succeeding volumes, such as *Buildings on Fire* (1900) and *Let Us Be as the Sun* (1903), added to Balmónt's reputation for possessing a sense of form and richness of rhythm almost unique among Russian poets. But in his voluminous later works, both original and translations, the richness began to cloy and the patterns of sound became monotonous.

Bryúsov and Balmónt were more interested in the language of poetry than in its content, and their symbolism was more a matter of theory than practice. With this movement, however, were soon associated a group of writers, some of them of remarkable talent, who brought a subtle intellection and at times a profound philosophical quality to the literature of symbolism. Zinaída Híppius reveals in both her prose and poetry a fondness for abstract ideas and an unusual skill in psychological observation. A more flawless and delicate symbolist poet was I. F. Ánnenski (1855–1909), whose *The Cypress Chest,* published in 1910, a year after his death, contains a small collection of lyrics that for compression, subtleness, and precision were scarcely equaled by any of the other symbolist writers. Almost a creative effort is required to master the thought of these perfect little poems, but once mastered, the thought seems ever fresh and enduring.

Ánnenski was a classical scholar of some note, but he failed to make the Greek spirit as definite a part of his intellectual equipment as did a still greater Greek scholar and contemporary symbolist poet—Vyacheslav Ivánov (1866–). The mystic religions of Greece have left their mark on Ivánov's thought in a curious identification of Christ and Dionysus. Like most of the symbolists, he welcomed the Revolution of 1905 and became the prophet of a new revolutionary philosophy that has been popularly denominated "Mystical Anarchism." In a Dostoyévskian sense Ivánov preached a non-acceptance of the world that amounted to a revolt against all external conditions and a demand that the spirit be completely emancipated. Between 1905 and 1911 Ivánov remained the leader of the Petersburg symbolists, opposing his doctrine that art was a mystical religious activity to that of the Moscow symbolists, headed by Bryúsov, who believed that the autonomy of art must be preserved against religion and philosophy. His best verse is contained in two volumes, *Cor Ardens* (1911), in which the ornate style reaches a high degree of perfection. Ivánov's poetic language has a carefully-wrought Byzantine richness about it, and the prevailing subject-matter is metaphysical. After the 1917 Revolution, he accepted the new order and lent his great talents to the communist cause.

Of the symbolist writers already mentioned, all had enjoyed the educational and cultural advantages of upper middle-class families. One of the most remarkable authors in the whole symbolist movement, and one of the most refined poets of the earlier group, came from the lower class and made his way to fame under trying material circumstances. He was Sologúb, whose real name was F. K. Tetérnikov (1863–1927). Although he began writing both prose and poetry in the early 1880's, he did not receive widespread recognition until the publication of his extraordinary novel, *The Little Demon*, in 1907. Sologúb's peculiar Manichean attitude towards life, in which he rejected the visible world as something inexpressibly vulgar for an ideal world of beauty of his own creating, is fully revealed in this novel. In *The Little Demon* the real world is depicted as one of incredible misery and squalor, fearfully symbolized by the hero Peredónov, one of the most striking characters in Russian fiction since Dostoyévsky. Other novels followed, and also short stories and plays, but the essence of the opposition between Sologúb's ideal heaven and the evil diversity of the real world in which

THE SYMBOLIST MOVEMENT

he lives is most beautifully and compellingly reflected in his poetry. Unlike the technique of the other symbolists, his vocabulary, diction, and metres are traditional, though employed with precision and felicity, but he uses words as symbols in which the secondary and not the ordinary meaning is consistently emphasized. There is a world of suggestiveness in his verse; it is poetry that requires the most careful reading, but the effort is amply repaid.

Perhaps the most original and at the same time the most difficult of the symbolists was Andréi Bély, whose real name was Borís Bugáyev (1880-1934). His versatility —he was a poet, novelist, essayist, and critic—seems to have prevented the concentration that might have resulted in supremely great achievement in any one of the several literary fields he essayed. Both Gógol and Dostoyévsky influenced him, but in his characteristic combination of mysticism and humor, Bély's real literary godfather was Vladímir Solovyóv, an influence later complicated by his devotion to Rudolf Steiner's anthroposophy. Bély's symbolism is expressed through a curious combination of two planes of existence, the actual and the fantastic or irrational. He dissociates reality, changes its proportions, and then substitutes for it a weird, subjective world of his own that is a blend of naturalism and apocalyptic mysticism, in the realization of which Bély often indulges in delightful flights of humor. Although notable as a poet, particularly for his metrical experiments (he is one of the foremost theorists on prosody in Russian), his most important contributions are in prose fiction. A series of novels, starting with *The Silver Dove* (1910), and followed by *Petersburg* (1913) and *Kótik Letáyev* (1920), to mention only the more notable productions, reveals Bély as an unusually original novelist. The direction of his fiction varies from the most difficult philosophical and symbolic writing to a clear Tolstóyan realism, and his style, in its most extreme form, has some of the characteristics of James Joyce's later prose.

An author that is often associated with Bély, both as a symbolist and a prose stylist, is A. M. Rémizov (1877–). One phase of his creative process is thoroughly dominated by a profound knowledge of native folk legends and tales; much of his writing is devoted to this subject matter and its treatment is profoundly influenced by *skaz,* that is, a language based on the living speech of the folk. The other important aspect of his creative process is his realism as exemplified by his novels. Such tales as *The Story of Stratilátov* (1909), an account of provincial life with some striking character creations, and *The Fifth Pestilence* (1912), another story of provincial life in all its ugliness, are written in a rich, ornamental, and highly mannered prose. Later novels, such as *Ólya,* are deliberately simple in style. In much of his fiction he subjects human fate to irrational forces in the manner of Dostoyévsky, and cunningly blends the real with the unreal. In his handling of themes he is extremely original, but his most important contribution and that in which he has been most influential, is his style. Like Bély, he applies to his prose the infinite care that is customarily applied to poetry, and the results have had a powerful influence on the prose of succeeding writers of fiction.

THE SYMBOLIST MOVEMENT

A younger poet who has eschewed the metrical patterns of the older symbolists but has appropriated the peculiar symbolic flavor of their subject matter is V. F. Khodasévich (1886–1939). His first book of verse in 1908 was little noticed, and it was not until his later works, such as *The Way of Grain* (1920) and *The Heavy Lyre* (1923), that he achieved widespread recognition and the reputation of a mature and skillful artist. His poetry happily combines mysticism and an ironic wit, not entirely unlike the verse of that older writer, Vladímir Solovyóv. In a style that is classical, almost as pointed and epigrammatic as that of the best writers of the Golden Age of Púshkin, he treats the theme of the eternal contradiction between the freedom of the soul and its submission to human necessity.

Two clear directions had been manifesting themselves in symbolist literature. The first, an aesthetic direction, emphasized refinement of form; the second emphasized religious-mystical feelings and the creation of dream worlds that were often realistically envisaged. Both these tendencies fuse in the works of the greatest of the symbolist poets, A. A. Blok (1880–1921). His first volume of poetry, *Verses about the Beautiful Lady* (1904), contained the history of the poet's mystical "love affair" with a person identified with Sophia, the Divine Wisdom, a feminine hypostasis of the Deity, the subject of Solovyóv's *Three Meetings*. The meaning evades anyone who is not well versed in the mystical experiences of Blok, but the verbal music of this volume revealed a poet of consummate technique. In the second volume of his collected verse, written between 1904 and 1908, Blok's mystical mistress deserts him and is replaced by an obsession for a strange woman who haunts his dreams. The poet in his disillusionment turns to more earthy and material themes, many of them effectively handled in a characteristic combination of realistic irony and romantic lyricism. Meanwhile Blok had undergone the despair of so many of the symbolist writers who had embraced the 1905 Revolution and then witnessed its hope turned to ashes in the reaction that followed. Some of his terrible pessimism finds expression in his two fine lyrical dramas, *The Puppet Show* and *The Stranger* (1906-1907). Wine, women, and song now begin to play a prominent part in his verse, and no doubt the lost vision of the "Beautiful Lady" of his mystical experience had something to do with the atmosphere of black despair and foreboding that clouded so much of his subsequent poetry.

Blok reached his poetical maturity about 1908. Lyrics and longer pieces of great power followed, in which one occasionally obtains a glimpse of a new love—a love of Russia. With this new love came a dawning political consciousness that manifested itself fitfully in between lengthening periods of despair. After the 1917 Revolution he found himself on the side of the Soviets, like Bryúsov and Bély, but perhaps for different reasons, for Blok saw in the revolt a great cleansing fire that would purify the soul of Russia. And this conception of the Communist Revolution found expression in his greatest poem, *The Twelve* (1918), a miracle of revolutionary mysticism and metrical harmony. The twelve in the poem are twelve Red Guardsmen who patrol the streets of Petrograd in a bitter snowstorm during the winter of 1917–1918. They swagger

THE SYMBOLIST MOVEMENT

along, "without the cross," jibing at the bourgeois, quarreling among themselves over a girl, and justifying all with their newly found "freedom, freedom." The background of the storm with its wind and snow sounds throughout the poem like an ominous revolutionary litany. The twelve Red Guardsmen symbolize the Twelve Apostles, and in the end Christ dramatically appears to lead them on their way. Shortly after this tremendous effort, Blok wrote one more poem, *The Scythians,* a fierce attack against the nations of Western Europe for their failure to heed the cry of the Bolsheviks for peace. Blok's revolutionary enthusiasm and poetic fervor now gave way again to his chronic despair and passive gloom, and he died three years later (1921), his fame secure as perhaps the greatest Russian poet since Lérmontov.

CHAPTER VII

The Revolution of 1917

THE TWELVE of Blok was in a sense the swan song of symbolism. Blok's own development led him from the abstract in symbolism to the actuality of life. As early as the winter of 1912–1913 new forces began to appear. Two symbolists, Sergéi Gorodétski (1884–) and N. S. Gumilyóv (1886–1921), issued a manifesto, in which they declared a revolt against the "mists, shadowy forms, and vague outlines" of symbolism, and announced their intentions to "sing the praise of the living world." A new school was formed, called "The Acmeists." The three chief disciples were Gumilyóv, a poet of genuine power, and his wife (for a short time) Anna Akhmátova (1895–), who wrote brief autobiographical poems, notable for their vivid realism and chiseled language, and O. E. Mandelstám (1892–), a poet who laid much stress on form.

Further opposition to symbolism appeared in the declarations and poetry of still another school at this time—the futurists. Igor Severyánin (1887–1942) was one of the earliest in the field, quickly followed by Velemír Khlébnikov (1885–1922) with his savage onslaughts on grammar and syntax, and the immensely talented V. V. Mayakóvski

THE REVOLUTION OF 1917

(1893-1930), who overwhelmed his readers with manifestoes that demanded the destruction of all literary traditions in the name of a new flesh-and-blood art that would do away with the pale aestheticism of the symbolists and the dry academism of the classics. The poetic program of the original futurist, the Italian Marinetti, was adopted by the Russians with their own variations: verse must now celebrate the modern era of the metropolis, of telephones, cinemas, aeroplanes, and skyscrapers, and it must do it with a special "wireless imagination" and in a style emancipated from the confining fetters of syntax and punctuation.

Meanwhile Russia was plunged into the First World War, which had little immediate effect upon the course of literary development. Authors kept singularly aloof from the struggle, and national patriotism soon waned under the impact of Court scandals, administrative incompetence, corruption, lack of food, and a loss of faith in the integrity of Russia's allies. In these circumstances, the February Revolution of 1917 that overthrew the monarchy aroused general enthusiasm, which had little time, however, to be reflected in literature. For the Bolshevik October Revolution that quickly followed and resulted in the defeat of the Provisional Government was pregnant with all the dark forces of civil war.

The fratricidal struggle lasted from 1917 to 1920, and during these terrible years widespread material privations and the lack of any means of publication almost completely interrupted literary production. Since long prose works were out of the question, poetry was nearly the only literary fare. And much of this was scribbled on scraps of paper and publicly recited by poets to half-fed and half-clothed gatherings in cafés. The man who sprang into sudden fame at this time was Mayakóvski, the futurist, but now he had boisterously accepted the Revolution and roared forth to bewildered listeners a poetry filled with fierce slogans that glorified the proletariat and condemned the bourgeoisie and their effete literature. He became the poetic mouthpiece of the new socialist order and worked out poster-like platform verses that served a powerful propagandist purpose.

Mayakóvski's principal rival was Sergéi Yesénin (1895–1925), a peasant by birth, whose marriage to Isadora Duncan brought him perhaps more international fame than his verse. Between 1923 and 1925 a veritable cult of "Yeséninism" existed and was frowned upon by local Communists as inimical to revolutionary ideals. Yesénin had begun his literary career in Petrograd as early as 1915, when he came under the influence of symbolist poets and later the imagists. But he soon struck his own original vein in poetry that celebrated the joys of village life in simple unsophisticated language. Epic attempts, such as *Pugachyóv*, failed, for his gift was essentially lyrical. Yesénin's initial enthusiasm for the Revolution quickly waned when he discovered that in the new order the paradise of the peasant must first give way to the dictatorship of the proletariat and the apotheosis of industry. The poems written during his bohemian existence in 1922–1923 (*The Tavern Moscow, The Confession of a Hooligan,* and *The Black Man*) range from "hooligan poems" of coarse aggressiveness to lyrics of ineffable sweetness on commonplace

THE REVOLUTION OF 1917

themes. His dramatic suicide in 1925, with a farewell poem written in his own blood, tells a tragic story of failure to adjust to a new way of life demanded by a new revolutionary morality.

The animosities of civil strife and the dawning conviction that the old order had passed forever soon forced nearly all writers to take sides in the bitter struggle. Of the older generation Búnin, Andréyev, Kúprin, Shmelyóv, Merezhkóvski, Híppius, Mínski, Bély, Severyánin, Rémizov, Balmónt, A. N. Tolstóy, and Marína Tsvetáyeva emigrated. A. N. Tolstóy, Bély, and later Kúprin and Tsvetáyeva returned. Indeed, few of the older writers elected to remain in Russia. Serafimóvich, Sergéyev-Tsénski (1876–), and Veresáyev stayed behind and continued to write; Bryúsov joined the Communist Party but was never happy in his allegiance and died in 1924; and Blok embraced the Revolution, but he too lived only a short time after it.

Out of the confusion and conflicting literary demands during the period of revolution and civil war, certain definite tendencies began to manifest themselves. Marxian critics demanded that a communist culture should be developed that would reflect the political, social, and economic ideals of the new proletarian régime, and the hope was freely expressed that this new culture would play a significant part in the world communist revolutionary movement. In 1920 the organization of the "Proletcúlt" was founded, the purpose of which was to direct the struggle for a proletarian culture on an international scale. Young poets and writers from among the workers were encouraged by every means and had the influential support of such important individuals as Lénin, Trótsky, Górky, and Lunachárski. Yet these young proletarian writers failed to produce anything outstanding. At the time this failure did not seem to matter much, provided the content of the literature served a revolutionary purpose. The spiritual struggle and tragic sense of futility of the old literature of the intelligentsia were banished and were replaced by a brave acceptance of life and a practical activism.

In their insistence upon the social tasks and duties of the new proletarian literature, however, the "Proletcúlt" authors fell into hopeless wrangling over means and ends. Two schools of thought arose. The moderate school, supported by Trótsky, Lunachárski, and the critic Vorónski, argued that it was impossible to create a proletarian literature by government fiat, and that at first much that was of value could be learned from the old bourgeois art and culture. The extremists, known as the "On Guard" group, frankly favored the idea of literary dictatorship, and demanded a definite class-literature. They were supported by Mayakóvski's LEF (Left Front) group. For a time the moderates won out. One fortunate result of this policy was that the pages of the new periodicals were opened to the non-political members of still another group, the "Serapion Brothers," founded in 1921. Most of these writers were intellectuals and capable of producing work of high artistic value, but they insisted upon the creative freedom of the individual. The more prominent among them were E. I. Zamyátin, K. Fédin, Vsévolod Ivánov, N. Tíkhonov, V. Kavérin (Zílberg), and M. Zóshchenko. At the same time other young authors, who, like the "Serapion Brothers," accepted the Revolution as an accomplished fact, although they did not personally adhere to communism, were encouraged to produce by the new dispensation. On the other hand, they were not hostile to the new order, and later most of them definitely accepted it. Trótsky labeled them "fellow-travelers" (*popútchiki*), and their efforts, particularly those of Borís Pilnyák, Leoníd Leónov, and V. Katáyev, helped materially in inaugurating the first positive step forward in Soviet literature.

CHAPTER VIII

The Beginnings of Soviet Fiction

THIS first advance manifested itself mostly in fiction and coincided with the period of the N. E. P. (New Economic Policy, 1921–1925). It was almost inevitable that this initial phase should deal with the wealth of material provided by revolution and civil war. Stirring events of violence and adventure, many of them lived by the young writers themselves, were eagerly seized upon by Pilnyák, Bábel, Fadéyev, Vsévolod Ivánov, Fúrmanov, and Fédin, to mention some of the more distinguished novelists. As a suitable medium for such thrilling themes, a dynamic prose was developed, not uninfluenced, however, by the stylistic inventiveness of the older writers Bély and Rémizov. In many cases this rich material from real life so beggared the imagination that what was most needed was an unobtrusive style adapted to fact and not to artistic invention. In truth, some of these accounts of real adventures were often written in a purely documentary style. One of the earliest works to attract attention for its gruesome depiction of revolutionary violence was *A Bare Year* (1922) of Borís Pilnyák (pseud. of B. A. Vogau, 1894–). Pilnyák is attracted more by the chaos and barbaric actions let loose by revolution than by its hopeful ideology. His romantic love of the elemental and dislike of sophisticated city existence with its industrial life as exhibited in succeeding novels, such as *Wolves and Machines* (1923) and *Mother Damp Earth* (1925), offended communist critics. His novel *Mahogany* (1927) only served to increase official opposition to him, which he tried to mitigate in later works.

One of the most brilliant of the early writers on civil war themes is Vsévolod Ivánov (1895–). At first he concentrated his efforts mostly on depicting guerilla warfare in Siberia in *Armored Train* (1922) and *Partisans* (1923). His civil-war characters are vivid and real, primitive in their emotions and actions, and he has a gift for handling mass scenes. Later works, such as *North Steel* (1925) and *The Mystery of Mysteries* (1927), are more tendentious and display deeper psychological power.

Another able painter of the romantic side of civil war is Dmítri Fúrmanov (1891–1926), whose best book *Chapáyev* (1923) is an authentic document of a peasant who became the popular commander of a whole division and saved Uralsk from the White forces. The hero is thoroughly realized in a work that has as much of the aspect of history as of imaginative literature. Also dealing with authentic material is Isaak Bábel's (1894–) *Red Cavalry* (1926), a collection of stories based on the author's experiences with Budyónny's Cossacks. These brief sketches are told with extraordinary concentration and a consummate mastery of the racy language of the Cossacks. War with all its cruelty and heroism, with its unbelievable coarseness and simple pathos, is unforgettably revealed.

On the whole, this early fiction dealing with revolution and civil war was concerned with forthright realistic or documentary narrative and avoided the psychological analysis of the old Russian masters. Although the initial tendency had been to condemn all literature of the past in building a new proletarian culture, the very leaders of the Communist Party stressed the need of learning from the best pre-revolutionary writers. And over this early period of the New Economic Policy novelists began to appear who treated themes connected with civil strife, but with a different emphasis and often in the traditional manner of Dostoyévsky, Tolstóy, and Chékhov.

Konstantín Fédin (1892–) was one of these authors, and his novel *Cities and Years* aroused great interest upon its appearance in 1924. It is an account of a Russian prisoner of war in Germany who returns to engage in revolutionary activity. The hero is a self-centered intellectual, however, and the story concerns his inner struggle, in which he eventually betrays the Revolution. Fédin treats revolution not as a glorious event, but as a profoundly disturbing psychological problem. His second long novel, *The Brothers* (1928), is quite similar in theme to *Cities and Years* and has very much the same involved construction in which chronology is sacrificed to dramatic narrative effects. The principal character, Nikíta Kárev, recalls the hero of *Cities and Years*, and like him is a returned prisoner of war from Germany. The background is the Revolution, and the hero, a musician, torn between the traditions of the old life and the demands of the new, fails in the end to find in music an adequate expression of the

Revolution and fails also in love. Fédin covers a vaster canvas and perhaps one which his talents are unequal to in his much-discussed novel, *The Rape of Europe*, which began to appear in 1934. The theme is the irreconcilable opposition between the capitalist West and socialist Russia. Fédin, much more so than most Soviet writers, has had considerable contact with the culture and countries of Western Europe, but this latest work tends to become a European travelogue, static in nature and unexciting in action. The best traits of Fédin's art—his character studies and original plot structure—are not well sustained in *The Rape of Europe*.

There is the flavor of Chékhov's Russia in Fédin's tales and of Dostoyévsky in the spiritual doubts of his heroes. Dostoyévsky's influence, however, is much more pronounced in the art of Leoníd Leónov (1899–), one of the most distinguished Soviet novelists. His early tale, *The End of an Insignificant Person* (1924), is a striking pastiche of Dostoyévsky. The story is built around a savant who starves to death during the famine period, and the question is raised whether the positive gains of a revolution justify the terrible wastage of human life and culture. In Leónov's first full-length novel, *The Badgers* (1925), a typical Dostoyévskian psychological approach is employed in the development of characters cast against a background of revolution. The theme is the fierce antagonism between town and village represented in two brothers, one a city-bred communist, the other a village *kulak*.

Leónov's tendency to blend analysis with the description of social events and their implied psychological problems became more pronounced in his later works. Critics praised his fiction as a bridge between Soviet realists and the classics of the past, a compliment that clearly indicated the bankruptcy of the early attempts to create a self-contained proletarian literature by laboratory methods. This link with the past is still more deeply rooted in A. N. Tolstóy (1883–), who had acquired literary fame before the Revolution. He was an émigré for several years, returned to Russia in 1921, and since then has achieved a position as one of the two or three foremost writers of the Soviet Union. One of his first works upon his return was *Aelita* (1922), a Wellsian novel, the action of which takes place on Mars. Of much more importance is his trilogy, *The Path of Suffering* (first part, 1921; the title of the English translation is *Darkness and Dawn*), in which he presents a picture of Russia before, during, and after the Revolution. The picture is authentic, most of the characters are thoroughly alive, and his language, as nearly always with A. N. Tolstóy, is most effective. His novel *Corn* (1937), a chronicle of the civil war in the Don and Volga regions, is less successful, although this work seems to mark the complete acceptance by the author of Soviet ideology. His later works are in full sympathy with the new régime.

Alexander Fadéyev's (1901–) first novel, *The Rout* (1926; translated into English as *The Nineteen*), betrays the obvious influence of Leo Tolstóy in its fresh realism and clear psychological insight. Like Vsévolod Ivánov, Fadéyev exploits his special knowledge of Siberia, for *The Rout* paints a broad, exciting picture of the civil war in that region. The work won him immediate fame, and he took a place

THE BEGINNINGS OF SOVIET FICTION

among the leading Soviet writers with his next and longest novel, *The Last of the Udegs,* which began to appear in 1929 (the last volume was published in 1935). Again the locale is Siberia and the main action concerns the civil war. But the background is more varied, for the author, apart from the main theme of showing the effect of revolution on a primitive nomadic tribe, the Udegs, also concerns himself with complex psychological problems connected with love, the family, and the hostile bourgeois spirit. Again the artistic method is Tolstóyan, a tradition that also worked its influence on another of the foremost Soviet novelists, Shólokhov, whose works, however, date from a slightly later period.

Revolution and civil war provided abundant material for a host of other fiction writers in this early period, but only the more prominent of them can be mentioned. There is the fine novel of Alexander Nevérov (1885–1923), *Tashként, The City of Plenty* (1922), that deals with the famine. Lýdia Seifúllina (1889–) caused something of a sensation by her novel *Manure* (1923), perhaps because of the striking naturalism with which she depicts the civil war on the border of Asia and the revivifying effect it had on a run-down community. *The White Guard* (1925) of Mikhaíl Bulgákov (1891–) concerns an episode in the civil war and portrays the Whites in a very sympathetic light. *The Lavróvs* (1927) of Mikhaíl Slonímski (1897–) is concerned with the effect of the Revolution upon intellectuals, and his later novel, *The Middle Avenue* (1928), depict the reaction of the lower middle class to the Revolution.

These writers of fiction in the early period of Soviet

literature vary in their technique, yet it is clear that a well-marked tendency to return to the traditional realistic manner began to increase after 1927. Some authors, however, were confessed followers of the modernistic, almost James Joycian, technique of Bély and Rémizov. Such, for example, was Artyóm Vesyóly (1899–), whose best-known works, *Native Land* (1927) and *Russia Washed in Blood* (1928), were strongly influenced by the folk-tale narrative style of Rémizov. And the same influence may be noted in the carefully wrought novel, *Kurymúshka* (1924), of the older writer Mikhaíl Príshvin (1873–).

CHAPTER IX

Fiction During the First Five-Year Plan

THE period of the New Economic Policy was succeeded by the first Five-Year Plan which Stálin inaugurated in 1928. The slogan was "Socialism in One Country," and again, as in the days of the "Proletcúlt," an attempt was made to regiment literature. A few interested communists, with the critic Áverbakh in the lead, seized control of the Russian Association of Proletarian Writers (RAPP) and laid down the uncompromising program that the depiction of the Five-Year Plan and of the class war within its framework was the only problem of Soviet literature. An extensive campaign was promulgated to execute their program, and all who refused to hew to the line found themselves outlawed. The results of this "planned literature" were for the most part unsatisfactory. Widespread discontent arose, and finally, in 1932, largely through the influence of Górky, a government edict dissolved the Russian Association of Proletarian Writers, and the literary dictatorship was brought to an end. A general Association of Soviet Writers was formed which was thrown open to all, for leading authorities expressed the belief that the majority of Soviet authors sympathized with the efforts of socialist construction, and hence it was pointless to demand of them outward proofs of their political loyalty. The extremists were defeated and once again the lesson was driven home that literature cannot flourish in chains.

The Five-Year Plan, however, provided plenty of material for fiction, and various writers treated it in various ways. Leónov, after his second novel, *The Thief* (1927), which dealt with the period of the New Economic Policy, turned his attention to socialist reconstruction in two novels, *Sot* (1930) and *Skutarévski* (1932). The first deals with the transformation of a northern wilderness into a busy center of the paper industry, and the second concerns a large-scale electrification task. Scientific technicalities abound in these tales of socialist reconstruction, but Leónov's characteristic Dostoyévskian concern for the "inner man" and his spiritual doubts over the blessings of the Revolution are everywhere in evidence. In his later novel, *The Road to the Ocean,* the hero for the first time in Leónov's works is a zealous communist, a fact that may symbolize that this fellow-traveler has at last fully accepted the new régime.

Another fellow-traveler, Pilnyák, took up the theme of reconstruction in his novel *The Volga Falls to the Caspian Sea* (1930). The plot involves the family tragedies of three engineers who are engaged in the task of diverting the course of a river, and the narrative is freely sprinkled with the technical details of construction, a practice that was generally adopted by the novelists of this period, and one that may have had an educative value but makes for hard reading The novel clearly suggests that Pilnyák found it hard to accept the vast industrialization program

FICTION DURING THE FIRST FIVE-YEAR PLAN

with enthusiasm. "I am not a Communist," he remarked once, "and therefore I do not believe that I must be a Communist and write like a Communist." His book *OK* (1933), based on a trip to America, was hardly appreciative, however, of the social scheme of things in this country. In his recent work, *The Ripening Fruits* (1938), he evinces for the first time what seems like a sincere enthusiasm for the aims of the Soviet régime.

One of the most laboriously documented novels of socialist reconstruction was F. V. Gladkov's (1883–) *Energy* (1933). He had previously written a highly popular novel, *Cement* (1926), that had described the zest with which the workers turned to social and economic reconstruction once the civil war had ended. *Energy* tells the story of Dnieprostrói and of the men and women who built the vast construction. What was intended to be a great human epic of socialist labor and triumph runs dangerously close to being simply the excessively detailed reporting of a tremendous feat of engineering.

Much better as a reconstruction novel was Valentín Katáyev's (1897–) *Time Forward!* (1933), which tells the story of shock brigades competing in the pouring of cement. The action consumes only twenty-four hours, and the narrative moves with verve and excitement, for Katáyev, one of the best Soviet novelists, is a master in depicting external action. In the form of this novel, one may clearly detect the influence of Dos Passos' fiction, which is much admired in Soviet Russia. While obvious sincerity, real joy, and justifiable pride were manifested in much of this fiction concerning the extraordinary accomplishments in the rapid industrialization of the country, a great many second-rate novels were turned out that pandered to the propaganda motifs of reconstruction at the expense of art. The unvarying pattern of communist workers frustrating the efforts of bourgeois wreckers grew monotonous and often stupid.

To this period also belongs the flowering of the genius of perhaps the greatest novelist in Soviet literature— Mikhaíl Shólokhov (1905–). Certainly he is the most read in Russia and his works are most widely known abroad. He began his long epic of Cossack life, *The Quiet Don* *(Quiet Flows the Don* in the English translation) in 1928– 1930. He interrupted it to write *Virgin Soil Upturned* (1932–1933), a novel dealing with the life of the new collective-farm Cossacks, and it is perhaps the best work on this popular theme of collectivization, although F. Panférov's 1896–) fine novel *Bruskí* (1930) will bear comparison with it. Shólokhov returned to his masterpiece, which was not finished until 1940. He is the most Tolstóyan of Soviet novelists. There is much of Tolstóy's epic sweep and his wonderful sense of realism in *The Quiet Don,* and Shólokhov's restraint and sense of proportion, his delicate handling of contrasts and parallels, and the simplicity of his character-drawing are qualities that remind one of Tolstóy. Finally, like Tolstóy, he is an uncompromising artist, independent and determined to go his own way.

In the whole development of fiction up to this point, there was no lack of criticism of Soviet life, a fact not commonly appreciated abroad. Satire was a favorite weapon, and although it was often directed against capitalist civilization, satire of the vices and foibles of Soviet life and the absurdities of Soviet officialdom was freely tolerated, provided it did not attack the fundamental ideals of the new order. Young Soviet authors learned from the older writer and satirist E. I. Zamyátin (1884–1937). He could never become reconciled to the Revolution, and his aversion to it was first manifested in his clever and powerful satire, *The Cave,* in which he likens the life of a bourgeois couple in their unheated room in Petrograd to the life of a paleolithic man in his cave. Subsequent satires, particularly his utopian novel *We* (1922–1924), a bitter satire on the equalizing tendencies of the Revolution, brought him into disfavor and he left the country.

Ilyá Ehrenbúrg (1891–) combines a clever vein of satire with a bright, attractive style. His shafts are aimed mostly against capitalist society, as in *The Extraordinary Adventures of Julio Hurenito* (1921). A skeptical, ironic nature runs through much of the prolific writings of Ehrenbúrg, and he is not above catering to popular tastes in his flair for topical themes and erotic situations. But there is also a deeply serious side to him, which has come out forcefully in his work as a correspondent in the Second World War and in his most recent book, *The Fall of Paris* (1942), in which he has presented, in fiction form, a brilliant picture of all those forces that contrived to betray France to Hitler.

The paradoxical reversion to a petty bourgeois existence in a communistic society that was brought about by the New Economic Policy provided irresistible material for satire. Bulgákov's *Devilry* (1925) poked fun, and not always good-natured fun, at Soviet life and Soviet bureaucracy. Katáyev's fine novel, *The Embezzlers* (1928), is a mordant satire on a pair of naively irresponsible state officials who steal a sum of money and roam about the country squandering their ill-gotten gains until they are caught and brought to justice.

Two of the most recently popular satirical and humorous writers and devoted collaborators have been Ilyá Ilf and Evgéni Petróv. (Ilf died in 1940 and Petróv was killed at the siege of Sevastopol in 1942.) Their satirical novels, *Twelve Chairs* (1927), *An Exalted Personage* (1928), and *The Golden Calf* (1933), were enthusiastically received, as well as their many amusing short stories of provincial life. Comic characters of the picaresque type and delightful adventures abound, and the collaborators distil the maximum of fun out of the foibles and vagaries of a swiftly changing Soviet life. A later book, *One Storeyed America*, contains the humorous reactions of a Soviet citizen to our capitalist society.

The most widely read Soviet humorist, however, is Mikhaíl Zóshchenko (1895–). An early member of the "Serapion Brothers," he lately has become a loyal supporter of the Soviet régime. More than ten volumes of his short stories have been published, the best of which are *A Merry Life* (1924), *Hard Times* (1926), *The Joyous Adventurer* (1927), *The Family Vitriol* (1930), and *The Reminiscences of Michél Sinyágin* (1932). Small incidents and comic trifles are the themes he most often deals with, but beneath the humor there is always latent a deft criticism of the abuses, foibles, and vices of Soviet life.

FICTION DURING THE FIRST FIVE-YEAR PLAN

During the period of the Five-Year Plan, and even earlier, novelists by no means neglected those vitally real ethical problems that arose from the conflict of the new communist conscience and ideals with the traditional views on sex, love, marriage, and the family. Such problems concern S. N. Sergéyev-Tsénski (1876–), a writer of the old school who has become a prominent Soviet novelist. The transition from bourgeois Russia to the new Soviet society is the principal theme of his series of ambitious novels under the title *Transfiguration* (first volume, 1923). With a somewhat similar theme in mind, Panteleimón Románov (1884–1936) designed a series of novels under the general title of *Russia*, but he soon abandoned this larger project for separate novels on less complicated aspects of the early period of Soviet life. Such is his *Comrade Kulyakóv*, translated into English under the title, *Three Pairs of Silk Stockings*, in which he draws a picture of the moral disintegration brought about among intellectuals by the Revolution. Yúri Libedínski (1898–) also addresses himself to ethical and social problems, especially in his best work, *The Birth of a Hero* (1930), in which he writes of love, family, and education in Soviet society.

Some of the older writers of fiction have practised their art abroad as émigrés, but their works, which on occasion have been translated into English, are naturally bare of the stuff of Soviet life. M. A. Osorgín (pseud. of Ilyín, 1878–1942) attracted considerable attention by his novel *Sivtsev Vrázhek* (translated into English as *Quiet Street*, 1930), a realistic novel of Russian life during the early years of the Revolution. *My Sister's Story* (1931), also translated into English, received less notice. More notable as a novelist is B. K. Záitsev (1881–) whose voluminous works are cast in the spirit of Turgénev, but have nothing of the fine sense of measure of the master. Turgénev's "superfluous" men reappear as the "superfluous" intellectuals (*The Golden Pattern*, 1925), who could not find their way in the battle of life after the Soviet Revolution. A fine lyric strain, compounded of impressionism and mysticism, runs through his fiction. The lyric strain is particularly strong in *Anna* (1929), a short novel—and one of the author's finest—about a sensitive girl who lives on her uncle's farm in an isolated corner of Soviet Russia. In this work Záitsev attemps to portray, although not very successfully, representatives of the new régime. A later piece, *Gleb's Journey*, the first part of which appeared in 1935, gives promise of being the best artistic effort of Záitsev.

Another émigré is M. A. Aldánov (pseud. of Lándau, 1886–) who is best known in English for his tetralogy of historical novels that deals with eighteenth-century subjects—*Saint Helena, Little Island* (1923), *The Ninth Thermidor* (1923), *The Devil's Bridge* (1925), *The Conspiracy* (1927). His portraits of Robespierre, Catherine II, Suvorov, and Paul I are drawn in the best tradition of Russian realism, and with just enough skepticism to impart the humility of common sense when historical greatness becomes both tiresome and unreal. Perhaps his finest work, however, is *The Tenth Symphony* (1931), which recreates Beethoven and the Vienna of his time—a symbolic tale of disillusion and unfulfilment. Aldánov has a superb gift for historical fiction, for he never allows the novelist's art to be subordinated to the bric-a-brac of documentation. Of late, he has turned his attention in fiction to the contemporary scene.

Younger than Aldánov is V. V. Nabókov (Russian pseud., Sírin, 1899–), who in a sense represents a new literary generation of Russian émigrés, for he has lived most of his life abroad, and lately has even taken to writing in English. A brilliant originality and a rare sensitiveness characterize much of his fiction, as *Lúzhin's Defence* (1930), the story of the progressive deterioration and final suicide of a chess prodigy, and *Invitation to an Execution* (1938), a macabre fantasy.

CHAPTER X

Soviet Poetry

IN the early days of the Revolution, Mayakóvski and his followers rang the death-knell of symbolism which had already run its full course. But the futurism that displaced symbolism soon betrayed its inadequacies as an artistic credo for revolutionary poets. The "roars and growls" of Mayakóvski quickly served their purpose and the ear became deafened. The telegraphic language and wireless imagination of the futurists baffled the proletariat. Their poetry had little in common with Marxism, and their insistence upon condemning the great classic poets of Russia's past to be lined up against the wall, like White generals, and shot, sounded hollow once the initial fury of the Revolution had spent itself. Lénin, the realist, gave the lie to these maudlin murderers of literary tradition when he candidly remarked: "I understand Púshkin and appreciate both him and Nekrásov, but as to Mayakóvski, I am sorry, I do not understand him." Mayakóvski eventually learned his lesson. He abandoned his poetic excesses, the studied vulgarity of his pre-revolutionary poem, *The Cloud in Trousers* (1915), and the bombast of *150,000,000* (1920) and brought his muse down to the proletarian earth, turning his great talents with a will to the service of the Revolution. He wrote poems about bread prices, the New Economic Policy, the food supply, and international events, or, as in *Vladímir Ilých Lénin,* he grasped an epic subject in stirring but simple language. Verse, he felt, must be turned into a kind of social function with the sole purpose of serving the Soviet state. He declared war on sensibility, meditation, and tenderness, and no doubt his denying these qualities, which were a genuine part of his nature, contributed to the disillusionment that helped to bring about his unfortunate suicide in 1930.

By insisting upon the communal function of verse, Mayakóvski exercised a powerful influence on subsequent poetry. His demand that Soviet poets participate in social creation and life was enthusiastically accepted by many younger writers, but none of these followers could equal the effectiveness of his message, and certainly none possessed the unique dynamism of his rhythms.

The poetry of this first period after the Revolution was declarative, spacious in its ideas, and given to abstract heroics. Soon the poets, like the novelists, were split into various factions by the conflicting demands made upon them by authority, communist conscience, and socialist needs. But poets found their way out of these controversies with much more difficulty than the writers of fiction. The complicated questions of form and poetics in general were stumbling blocks not easily surmounted by the young untrained peasant and proletarian poets who came to the fore. Many of them, in the words of Bezyménski, sought "to discover the world revolution in every detail," and they often lost themselves and their art in the process. Unlike fiction, Soviet poetry, except for the works of a few first-rate artists, remained for an excessively long time in a transitional stage. In the struggle between rationalism and emotionalism, mere affirmation of faith unsupported by the poets' convictions and imaginative vision leads to a reiteration of banalities no less flat than those in the bourgeois verse these young Soviet poets so fiercely condemned.

The real early poet-laureate of the Revolution was not Mayakóvski, but Demyán Bédny (pseud. of Yefím A. Pridvórov, 1883–), a "Bolshevik whose weapon is poetry," as Trotsky described him. Much of his verse (there are more than fifteen volumes of it) consists of satirical and humorous commentaries on daily events in Soviet life. A good deal of his work hardly rises above the level of doggerel, but the best of it has the authentic ring of genuine folk poetry.

One of the earliest proletarian poets to attract notice was A. K. Gástev (1882–), whose book of verse in 1918 contained poems devoted to the beauties of machines and to the lofty future of industrialism. Another early proletarian poet was M. P. Gerásimov (1889–), who published a number of collections of verse between 1917 and 1924. And two early peasant poets of the Revolution were N. A. Klyúyev (1889–), who hailed the new order and its great leader Lénin in unusually finished verse, and P. V. Oréshin (1887–), whose three volumes of collected verse (1923–1927) won him considerable popularity as a poet of the social revolution.

SOVIET POETRY

The young writers who were most immediately influenced by Mayakóvski liked to think of themselves as proletarian poets, although their connection with the working class was often tenuous indeed. They began to flourish after 1923, and by far the most popular of them for a time was A. I. Bezyménski (1898–). For all these younger proletarian poets, devotion to the Communist Party took precedence over devotion to the muse. In bombastic verse that had about as much musicality as a loud yawp, Bezyménski arrogantly dismissed the past—Dante was simply "that son of a bitch"—and geared his numbers to proletarian realities, as in one of his early works, *That's How Life Smells* (1924). As he gathered experience, the Party and political propaganda were used less ostentatiously as themes, and a growing realization of the sterner tasks confronting the socialist régime began to creep into his verse (*Pathways*, 1925; *The Shot*, 1929; and *Poems About Love*, 1932).

Among this group of proletarian poets, Alexander Zhárov (1904–) is a paler and duller disciple of Mayakóvski; Nikolái Ushakóv (1899–) in his *The Spring of the Republic* is authentically Mayakóvskian but possesses a more lyrical strain; and Mikhaíl Golódny (1903–), Iván Dorónin (1900–), and Mikhaíl Svetlóv (1903–) are less proletarian in their themes and more romantic in their treatment of them. This is especially true of Svetlóv, who has written some talented poetry on subjects connected with the civil war. A proletarian poet with a larger vision and a richer talent than any of those already mentioned is Vasíli Kázin (1898–).

In his *Poems About Love,* Bezménski had condemned Mayakóvski's unsocial act of suicide, but Nikolái Aséyev (1889–) honored the dead master's memory in his long narrative poem, *Mayakóvski Emerges* (1940). Aséyev, one of the early futurists and followers of Mayakóvski, accepted the Revolution at its outset, and is now regarded as one of the best Soviet poets. His popularity rests largely on several long poems on revolutionary themes, in which he is always the romantic and full of life and vitality.

An offshoot of futurism was constructivism, a vague movement dedicated to subordinating the imagery and vocabulary of poetry to the theme. The principal theoretician is Kornély Zelínski (1896–) and the chief poet of the movement is Ilyá Selvínski (1899–). Selvínski is a realist who stresses the social function of poetry, and in several long verse tales he displays often the art of the novelist as much as that of the poet, but he is quite capable of lyric flights. Another constructivist, although many influences worked upon him, was Eduard Bagrítski (1895–1934) who died young. Highly talented and with a particularly fine lyric gift, he wrote on a large variety of themes, many of them having no relation to the Revolution, though there can be no doubt about his sympathies. His contacts with the constructivist poets were slight.

Borís Pasternák (1890–), who began to write under the influence of the futurists, is generally regarded as the foremost Soviet poet today. Essentially a lyric poet, his attempts at long verse narratives, such as *Spéktorski* (1926) and *The Year 1905* (1927), are not well sustained, although brilliant lyrical passages occur in them. Pasternák finds it

SOVIET POETRY

difficult to identify his muse with political and socialistic themes, although he has tried on occasion. For he is primarily an individualist—a highly cultured one—and a romantic, who writes with passionate intensity on the traditional subject of nature, which serves so often as a background for personal lyric utterances. His striking originality finds fullest expression in his language and poetic form. It is a difficult, elliptical, obscure language, with unorthodox syntactical turns, but the musical and rhythmical effects, built up on the intonations and cadences of ordinary speech, are wonderfully successful.

Pasternák's principal rival for top honors in Soviet poetry today is Nikolái Tíkhonov (1896–), although no discerning critic would think of comparing the two. Tíkhonov possesses neither the sheer poetic power nor originality of Pasternák. On the other hand, he is relatively free of the difficult language and complicated handling of themes that have prevented Pasternák from winning popularity among the widest circle of readers. It is not easy to place Tíkhonov in any particular poetic school, for since the time of his early narrative verse tales (*The Horde*, 1921, and *Mead*, 1922) to his later ballads on civil-war themes and his recent poems, he has consistently and independently developed his art largely as a medium for treating romantic themes of revolution in a clear, realistic manner. At times, Tíkhonov seems more like a novelist in verse, and his simple, unstrained realism has influenced other poets, such as G. Lelévich (1901–), Semyón Ródov (1893–), and Sergéi Obradóvich (1892–).

It is clear that Soviet poetry in its performance has

lagged behind fiction, which has been pretty much the case in Western Europe and America over the last twenty years. The doubt, despair, and negation of so much of Western European verse, however, have been absent from the poetry of Soviet Russia. If anything, Soviet poetry has been characterized by an exuberance and an almost excessive determination to mirror life, albeit a socialistic life. In its efforts to condemn a whole world of emotive complexes and values, Soviet poetry inevitably became a literature of fierce conflicts and action. But the constant, driving change of the new life, which was more easily assimilated by fiction, has proved a deterrent to the healthy growth of poetry; for the development of poetry requires periods of calm and contemplation in order that forms may crystallize and faith may take root in the poetic consciousness. Most recent Soviet verse, however, bears a promise of greatness for the future; form is grasped with more sureness, and a clear vision of the socialist state lends inspiration where doubt and conflict had formerly confused and enervated positive affirmation.

CHAPTER XI

Soviet Drama

IT has become a critical commonplace to observe that the Soviet theatre is perhaps the finest in the world but that a comparable dramatic literature has failed to materialize. The names of famous theatres—the First Moscow Art, the Meyerhóld, the Vakhtángov, and the Kámerny—as well as their distinguished directors, sound more familiar to foreign ears than do the names of Soviet playwrights. And it seems almost as though foreign plays are performed more often than Russian ones, for there is hardly an important drama in world literature that has not appeared on the Soviet stage. Although it is true that the native repertoire has not kept pace with outstanding developments in the art of the theatre, yet on a comparative basis the whole corpus of Soviet plays written during the last twenty-five years is not markedly inferior in quantity or quality to that of any nation in the West or of America.

As in all Soviet literature, the drama has also faithfully reflected in its themes and treatment the rapid political, social, and economic changes that have taken place since the Revolution. The dramatists first upon the scene were mostly those who belonged to the intelligentsia and in some cases had practised their art before the Revolution, such as A. N. Tolstóy, K. A. Trénev (1878–), N. Érdman, A. V. Lunachárski, B. S. Romashóv (1895–), and S. M. Tretyakóv (1892–). Futuristic, romantic, and realistic tendencies are apparent in their plays, none of which, however, won any enduring success. Several other writers, a few of them primarily novelists, may be included in this group, and in some cases their dramatic efforts have earned a permanent place in Soviet repertoire. There are Bábel's *The Sunset* and *Maria;* Fédin's *Bakúnin in Dresden;* Leónov's adaption of his novel *Skutarévski;* Vsévolod Ivánov's dramatized novel, *The Armored Train,* a striking success; Seifúllina's *Virinéya;* Bulgákov's memorable *Days of the Turbins,* a dramatization of his novel, *The White Guard,* one of the best plays to come out of Soviet Russia, Katáyev's *Squaring the Circle,* a highly amusing comedy on Soviet marriage; and Yúri Olésha's *The Three Fat Men.*

A second group of dramatists, most of them peasant and proletarian writers, were concerned with propaganda plays, often crudely executed, and also with plays on the civil war and on subjects that grew out of the social problems raised by the Revolution, such as Nevérov's *The Womenfolk* (1923), Gladkóv's *The Band* (1932), and Bill-Belotserkóvski's *Echo* (1924) and *The Storm* (1926).

A third group of dramatists, to which belong young Soviet writers with a post-revolutionary training, have contributed plays of considerable merit. Among the best of these dramatists are A. N. Afinogénov (1904–1942),

SOVIET DRAMA

Vladímir Kirshón (1902–), V. V. Vishnévski (1901–), and N. F. Pogódin (1900–). As in fiction, the pronounced tendency of drama has been in the direction of realism, in which attempts were made to grapple with the conflicts induced by the swiftly changing tempo of Soviet life. People soon wearied of the forthright propaganda plays, such as Mayakóvski's bizarre *Mystery-Bouffe* (1918) and Tretyakóv's rather crude drama of imperialism, *Roar China!* (1926). A few of the civil-war plays, especially Ivánov's *Armored Train,* Bulgákov's *Days of the Turbins,* and Trénev's *Lyubóv Yarováya* (1926), were well constructed and strikingly realistic.

The Five-Year Plan was as prolific in plays as it was in novels, and a monotonous sameness attended both genres. Plays were formed to a stereotyped pattern and were often hopelessly and boringly didactic. The invariable theme was a bit of villainous wrecking on a construction job or on a collectivized farm, in which the counter-revolutionary plotters are foiled and the good communists triumphant. Afinogénov's fine drama *Fear* (1931) was an exception, although the usual counter-revolutionary conspiracy is present. But the play also attempts to solve in terms of individual and not mass psychology the significant moral problem of the Revolution's right to terror. Pogódin's *Tempo* (1930) and Kirshón's *Bread* (1933) were also much better than the average Five-Year-Plan plays, despite rather poor construction and careless language. And Olésha's *A List of Benefits* (1931), very much like Afinogénov's *Fear,* leaves room for the workings of individual psychology in dramatizing the conflict between individualism and socialism.

Most recent tendencies in Soviet drama in no sense lessen the emphasis upon realism, but they are running in the direction of a fuller comprehension of the individual's problems in a collectivist society. The socialist didactic element has by no means been eliminated, but there is a deeper searching into the cause and effect of universal human behavior. And coupled with this is an earnest concern with the Russian people as a whole, unconditioned by time, a tendency that is reflected in historical plays and in the dramatic adaptations of great novels of the past, such as Tolstóy's *Anna Karénina* and *War and Peace*.

CHAPTER XII

Recent Trends In Soviet Literature

WORLD WAR II awakened us to the fact that there was much about Soviet Russia that we did not know, and that some things we thought we knew were erroneous. Yet odd notions still exist concerning the state of Soviet literature. The excesses of the youthful period of the Revolution still linger in the minds of foreigners: the fierce condemnation of all the great classics of the past; the strident demands for new forms, new content, and new values; and the determination to expunge artistic individualism and to club literature into the service of the State. But meanwhile Soviet Russia has matured, without the rest of the world knowing or caring to know. Hardly any nation today devotes more attention to the study of the great literary monuments of the past. A mature sense of responsibility to the reading public actuates both authors and government. The vast population has become literary-minded, and the demand for books exceeds that of perhaps any other country.

More sympathetic understanding than critical explanation is required in order to grasp the real significance of the development of Soviet literature. Ever since its existence Soviet Russia has been in an almost constant state of emergency, and it has been this fact that has often dictated the frequent radical changes and sharp reverses in the life and culture of the country. On the surface there was always an abiding impermanency. The more permanent values and universal constants of human behavior, however, were never very far beneath the surface of the continual flux, and this was quite true in the swiftly changing literary trends. The highly specialized communist conscience in the novels, let us say, of Nikolái Ostróvski (1904–1936)—*Those Born by the Storm* (1936) and *How the Steel was Tempered* (1937)—could give way to ethical and idealistic trends, to the universal emotions and values that transcend all classes, in the works of a score of other novelists. For example, Sergéi Maláshkin (1890–) bravely ponders in his fiction (*The Moon on the Right-Hand Side,* 1927) the difficult emotional complexities of his generation; Sergéi Budántsev (1896–) startled the reading public by going outside Soviet Russia for the hero of his *Tale of a Suffering Mind* (1931)—a philosopher and scientist of the 1860's who distrusts the easy panaceas of his day in his search for the meaning of existence; and Yúri Olésha (1899–) in his much-discussed novel *Envy* (1927), written in an impressionistic style, frankly faced the problem of the personal emotions and inclinations of Soviet citizens in conflict with imposed systems. Still another defender of spiritual independence and individual freedom is the gifted Veniamín Kavérin (1902–), in such novels as *The Anonymous Artist* (1931) and *The Fulfillment of Wishes* (1934–1935).

RECENT TRENDS IN SOVIET LITERATURE

Thus one may discern in recent trends distinct links with the past, for social idealism, as well as an interest in the human soul, had been pronounced aspects in the literary production of the old intelligentsia. Even the historical novel, of which the past furnished some few brilliant examples, has taken on the proportions of a widespread movement in Soviet Russia, as it has in America recently. The tendency of foreign critics to dismiss this eager interest in the historical past as an enforced escape from dangerous contentious themes of the present is hardly justified. It is only natural that Soviet writers should desire to apply their dialectic method to reinterpreting the past in the light of the present. The method is usually the brutal realistic one, devoid of any sentimental romancing, that has been used so successfully in writing on the civil war, and in most cases the documentation is extraordinarily full.

Peter I (1929–1934) of A. N. Tolstóy is one of the finest of these Soviet historical novels. He treats the period of the great tsar as one of transition, not unlike that of present-day Russia, and one can see in the sympathetic portrait of Peter a forerunner of Lénin or Stálin. Where A. N. Tolstóy is largely deficient, namely in the psychology of his characters, another older writer, Sergéyev-Tsénski, admirably succeeds. Since his expansive novel on the Crimean War, *The Defense of Sevastopol,* he has recently embarked on a theme connected with the First World War —*The Brusílov Break-Through.*

Two other older writers have devoted themselves to historical fiction. Alekséi Chapýgin (1870–1937) has produced *Stépan Rázin* (1926-27), a thrilling tale of the 17th-century Russian Robin Hood, who is presented as a kind of early "Bolshevik" leader, but the authentic atmosphere and local color of Sténka Rázin's time are exactly recreated. The *Tsushima* (1934) of A. Nóvikov-Pribói (1877-) is on quite a different theme—a chronicle of the sinking of the Russian fleet in the Russo-Japanese War.

Yúri Tynyánov's (1894-) historical novels are concerned solely with literary figures of the past—*Kyúkhlya* (1925), a story of the pathetically comic Decembrist poet and friend of Púshkin, Küchelbecker; *The Death of Vazír Mukhtár* (1929), which tells the story of the famous dramatist, Griboyédov, in the early years of the 19th century; and *Púshkin* (1936), which portrays the early life of the great Russian poet. Tynyánov is more of a scholar than a novelist; his documentation is impeccable and the atmosphere of the past is admirably reproduced, but his characters come to life with difficulty. In these historical novels, and in many others of less note, one is impressed by the repeated emphasis upon the patriotic motif. It is not so much an arrant chauvinism or nationalism, but rather a glorification of the unity and heroism of the past that must be reborn in the present as a warning to the enemies of the socialist fatherland. For Soviet Russia was well aware of the dangers from without, and this note of patriotic warning against a definite enemy—Japan—was plainly sounded in P. Pavlénko's (1899-) novel *In the East* (1937).

A new force is apparent in Soviet literature which clearly sets it apart from the literature of any other country over the last twenty-five years. The total production, which has been enormous, is thoroughly penetrated by a social consciousness and a profound responsibility to the people. Despite the constant flux and new demands of the present, Soviet literature has many of its roots in the past, but it ceaselessly endeavors to integrate all the best elements of the past and present in an effort to create the vision of a glorious future.

The new note may perhaps best be described by the much-debated critical slogan, "socialist realism," that first appeared in 1932. However new the term, exponents of socialist realism existed in Russia long before the advent of the Soviets. For writers such as Belínski, Hérzen, Chernyshévski, and even Tolstóy, who believed that the individual and the community were not opposing but complementary factors in each other's well-being, were in a sense devotees of socialist realism. Of late, bourgeois realism has displayed a degree of defeatism, frustration, and pessimism that suggests a progressive disintegration of the modern society that it describes. With a loss of faith has come a loss of social consciousness, and the bourgeois writer tends to become self-centered and hostile to the community.

The difference between the Soviet realist and the bourgeois realist is essentially a difference between faith in life and lack of faith. The Soviet writer can be as fiercely realistic and critical as the bourgeois writer, but he is inspired by a different philosophy—he has a new faith in man. Behind his accurate description of reality is a desire to obtain a clearer understanding of all that must be abolished and all that must be built up. If there is tragedy in his works, there is no pessimism, for the dominant note is one of hope born of faith. Socialist realism attempts to integrate literature and life, to direct the creative present towards a more meaningful creative future. Soviet literature has scarcely begun to realize its vast potentialities, but its present vitality, positive affirmation, and soaring faith give promise of a great future.

A Selective Guide to Modern Russian Literature in English Translation (1880-1940)

ANTHOLOGIES AND COLLECTIONS

COURNOS, JOHN, compiler and translator. *Short Stories Out of Soviet Russia.* New York, E. P. Dutton, 1929. (Cited as "Cournos")
COXWELL, CHARLES F., translator. *Russian Poems.* London, C. W. Daniel, 1929. (Cited as "Coxwell")
DEUTSCH, BABETTE and AVRAHM YARMOLINSKY. *Russian Poetry.* New York, International Publishers, 1927. (Cited as "Deutsch")
FRIEDLAND, L. S. and J. R. PIROSHNIKOFF, translators. *Flying Osip: Stories of New Russia.* London, T. Fisher Unwin, 1925. (Cited as "Friedland")
GRAHAM, STEPHEN, editor. *Great Russian Short Stories.* New York, Liveright, 1929. (Cited as "Graham")
LYONS, EUGENE. *Six Soviet Plays.* Boston, Houghton Mifflin, 1934. (Cited as "Lyons")
MONTAGU, IVOR and HERBERT MARSHALL, editors. *Soviet Short Stories.* London, Pilot Press, 1942. (Cited as "Montagu")

MODERN RUSSIAN LITERATURE IN ENGLISH

NOYES, GEORGE R., compiler and editor. *Masterpieces of the Russian Drama.* New York, D. Appleton, 1933. (Cited as "Noyes")

PATRICK, GEORGE Z. *Popular Poetry in Soviet Russia.* Berkeley, Calif., University of California Press, 1929. (Cited as "Patrick")

REAVEY, GEORGE and MARC SLONIM, editors and translators. *Soviet Literature: An Anthology.* New York, Covici-Friede, 1934. (Cited as "Reavey")

ROBBINS, J. J., translator. *Azure Cities: Stories of New Russia.* New York, International Publishers, 1929. (Cited as "Robbins")

TRANSLATIONS—INDIVIDUAL
AUTHORS

AFINOGENOV, A. N. *Distant Point; a Play.* Trans. and adapted by Hubert Griffith. London, Pushkin Press, 1941.
—— *Fear.* Trans. by Charles Malamuth. (In Lyons, pp. 389–469)
—— *Fear.* Trans. by N. Strelsky, Dorothy Beach Colman, and A. Greene. Poughkeepsie, N.Y., Experimental Theatre of Vassar College, 1934.

AKHMATOVA, ANNA. *All Is Plundered.* (In Reavey, p. 350)
—— *Poems.* (In Coxwell, pp. 254–56; and Deutsch, pp. 155–58)

ALDANOV, M. A., *pseud.* See Landau, M. A.

ANDREYEV, L. N. *He Who Gets Slapped.* Trans. by Gregory Zilboorg. New York, Brentano's, 1922.

ANDREYEV, L. N. *Judas Iscariot.* (In *The Crushed Flower, and Other Stories.* Trans. by Herman Bernstein) New York, A. Knopf, 1916.
────── *The Life of Man.* (In *Plays.* Trans. by L. Meader and Fred Newton Scott) New York, Scribner's, 1915.
────── *Professor Storitsyn.* (In Noyes, pp. 739–99)
────── *The Red Laugh.* Trans. by A. Linden. New York, Duffield, 1915.
────── *The Seven That Were Hanged.* Trans. by Herman Bernstein. New York, J. S. Ogilvie, 1909.
────── *Silence.* Trans. by W. H. Lowe. London, F. Griffith, 1910.
ANNENSKI, I. F. *Poems.* (In Coxwell, pp. 189–91)
APUKHTIN, A. N. *Nights of Madness.* (In Coxwell, p. 185)
ARTSYBASHEV, M. P. *Breaking-point.* London, M. Secker, 1915.
────── *Jealousy.* New York, Boni and Liveright, 1923.
────── *The Millionaire.* Trans. by Percy Pinkerton. New York, B. W. Huebsch, 1915.
────── *Sanine.* Trans. by Percy Pinkerton. New York, Viking Press, 1926.
────── *The Savage.* Trans. by Gilbert Cannan and Mme. A. Strindberg. New York, Boni and Liveright, 1924.
────── *Tales of the Revolution.* Trans. by Percy Pinkerton. New York, B. W. Huebsch, 1917.
────── *War.* Trans. by Thomas Seltzer. New York, A. Knopf, 1916.
BABEL, ISAAK. *The Awakening.* (In Reavey, pp. 164–70)
────── *The End of Saint Ipaty.* (In Reavey, pp. 137–43)

MODERN RUSSIAN LITERATURE IN ENGLISH

BABEL, ISAAK. *Red Cavalry.* Trans. by Nadia Helstein. New York, A. Knopf, 1929.
BALMONT, KONSTANTIN. *Poems.* (In Coxwell, pp. 200–21)
——— *Poems.* (In Deutsch, pp. 96–9)
BEDNY, DEMYAN, *pseud.* See Pridvorov, Yefim.
BELY, ANDREI, *pseud.* See Bugayev, Boris.
BEZYMENSKI, ALEXANDER. *Poems.* (In Deutsch, p. 223)
——— *A Poem About Love.* (In Reavey, pp. 374–76)
——— *A Song About a Man.* (In Reavey, pp. 274–78)
BILL-BELOTSERKOVSKI, V. N. *Life Is Calling.* Trans. by A. Wixley. New York, International Publishers, 1939.
BLOK, A. A. *New America.* (In Reavey, pp. 336–38)
——— *Poems.* (In Coxwell, pp. 224–46)
——— *Poems.* (In Deutsch, pp. 141–47; 173–89)
——— *The Stranger.* (In Coxwell, pp. 225–26)
——— *The Twelve.* Trans. by Babette Deutsch and Avrahm Yarmolinsky. New York, W. E. Rudge, 1931.
——— *The Twelve* (excerpts). (In Reavey, pp. 338–39)
BRYUSOV, V. YA. *The Fiery Angel.* Trans. by Ivor Montagu and Sergei Nalbandov. London, H. Toulmin, 1930.
——— *Poems.* (In Deutsch, pp. 104–11)
——— *The Republic of the Southern Cross.* New York, McBride, 1919.
BUGAYEV, BORIS. *Kotik Letayev* (excerpts). (In Reavey, pp. 55–67)
——— *Poems.* (In Coxwell, pp. 222–23)
——— *Poems.* (In Reavey, p. 340)
BULGAKOV, MIKHAIL. *Days of the Turbins.* (In Lyons, pp. 1–85)

BUNIN, IVAN. *The Elaghin Affair.* Trans. by Bernard Guilbert Guerney. New York, A. Knopf, 1935.
—— *The Gentleman from San Francisco.* Trans. by Bernard Guilbert Guerney. New York, A. Knopf, 1934.
—— *Mitya's Love.* Trans. by M. Boyd. New York, Holt, 1926.
—— *Poems.* (In Deutsch, pp. 113-17)
—— *The Village.* Trans. by Isabel F. Hapgood. New York, A. Knopf, 1933.
—— *The Well of Days.* Trans. by Gleb Struve and Hamish Miles. New York, A. Knopf, 1934.
CHEKHOV, ANTON. *The Cherry Orchard.* (In Carl Van Doren, editor. *An Anthology of World Prose.* New York, Reynal and Hitchcock, 1935, pp. 1026-57)
—— *The Chorus Girl.* Trans. by Constance Garnett. New York, Macmillan, 1920.
—— *The Seagull.* Trans. by Constance Garnett. (In *The Plays of Anton Tchekov* [Chekhov]. New York, Modern Library, 1930)
—— *Stories of Russian Life.* Trans. by Marian Fell. New York, Scribner's, 1914.
—— *The Three Sisters.* Trans. by Clarence Garnett. London, Chatto and Windus, 1938.
—— *Uncle Vanya.* (In Ernst Watson, compiler. *Contemporary Drama,* New York, Scribner's, 1941, pp. 269-91)
EHRENBURG, ILYA. *The Extraordinary Adventures of Julio Jurenito and His Disciples.* Trans. by Usick Vanzler. New York, Covici-Friede, 1930.

EHRENBURG, ILYA. *The Love of Jeanne Ney.* Trans. by Helen Chrouschof Matheson. Garden City, N.Y., Doubleday, Doran, 1930.

——— *Out of Chaos.* Trans. by Alexander Bakshy. New York, Holt, 1934.

——— *The Sons of Our Sons.* (In Deutsch, pp. 196–97)

——— *A Street in Moscow.* Trans. by Sonia Volochova. New York, Covici-Friede, 1932.

FADEYEV, ALEXANDER. *The Last of the Udegs* (excerpts). (In Reavey, pp. 299–314)

——— *The Nineteen.* Trans. by R. D. Charques. New York, International Publishers, 1929.

FURMANOV, DMITRI. *Chapayev.* Moscow, Cooperative Publishing Society of Foreign Workers in the U.S.S.R., 1934.

GARSHIN, VSEVOLOD. *The Signal.* New York, A. Knopf, 1917.

GASTEV, A. K. *Poems.* (In Deutsch, pp. 210–12)

GERASIMOV, MIKHAIL. *The First Bulb Is Turned On.* (In Deutsch, p. 213)

——— *Poems.* (In Patrick, pp. 207–09)

GLADKOV, FYODOR. *Cement.* Trans. by A. S. Arthur and C. Ashleigh. New York, International Publishers, 1926.

GLEBOV, ANATOLI. *Inga.* Trans. by Charles Malamuth. (In Lyons, pp. 311–88)

GORKY, MAXIM. *Bystander.* Trans. by Bernard Guilbert Guerney. New York, D. Appleton-Century, 1930.

——— *Chelkash.* New York, A. Knopf, 1929.

GORKY, MAXIM. *The Confession.* Trans. by Rose Strunsky. New York, F. A. Stokes, 1916.

―― *Foma Gordeyev.* Trans. by Herman Bernstein. New York, Bee De Publ. Co., 1928.

―― *Fragments from My Diary.* London, P. Allan, 1924.

―― *In the World.* Trans. by Gertrude M. Foakes. New York, Century, 1917.

―― *The Life of Klim Samgin.* See *Bystander* (trans. 1930); *The Magnet* (trans. 1931); *Other Fires* (trans. 1933); *The Specter* (trans. 1938).

―― *The Lower Depths.* Trans. by Laurence Irving. New York, Duffield, 1912.

―― *The Magnet.* Trans. by Alexander Bakshy. New York, D. Appleton-Century, 1931.

―― *Mother.* New York, D. Appleton-Century, 1938.

―― *My Childhood.* New York, D. Appleton-Century, 1936.

―― *My University Days.* New York, Boni & Liveright, 1923.

―― *Other Fires.* Trans. by Alexander Bakshy. New York, D. Appleton-Century, 1933.

―― *The Specter.* Trans. by Alexander Bakshy. New York, D. Appleton-Century, 1938.

―― *Three of Them.* Trans. by A. Linden. London, T. F. Unwin, 1905.

―― *Twenty-Six Men and a Girl.* Edited by Avrahm Yarmolinsky and Baroness Moura Budberg. New York, Holt, 1939.

HIPPIUS, ZINAIDA. *Poems.* (In Deutsch, pp. 94-5)

―― *Poems.* (In Coxwell, pp. 202-04)

ILF, ILYA, and YEVGENI PETROV. *The Adventures of a Fakir.* New York, Vanguard Press, 1935.
—— *Diamonds To Sit On.* Trans. by Elizabeth Hill and Doris Mudie. New York, Harper, 1930.
—— *Little Golden America.* Trans. by Charles Malamuth. New York, Farrar & Rinehart, 1937.
—— *The Little Golden Calf.* Trans. by Charles Malamuth. New York, Farrar & Rinehart, 1932.
ILYIN, M. A. *My Sister's Story.* New York, Dial Press, 1931.
—— *Quiet Street.* New York, Dial Press, 1930.
IVANOV, VSEVOLOD. *Armored Train 14–69.* Trans. by Gibson-Cowan and A. T. K. Grant. New York, International Publishers, 1933.
—— *The 'Merican.* (In Friedland, pp. 114–20)
—— *On the Rails.* (In Friedland, pp. 121–29)
IVANOV, VYACHESLAV. *Poems.* (In Deutsch, pp. 118–27)
KATAYEV, VALENTIN. *The Embezzlers.* Trans. by L. Zarine. New York, Dial Press, 1929.
—— *Lonely White Sail; or, Peace Is Where the Tempests Blow.* Trans. by Charles Malamuth. London, Allen & Unwin, 1937.
—— *Squaring the Circle.* (In Lyons, pp. 85–154)
—— *Squaring the Circle* (Mercury Theatre version). Boston, W. H. Baker, 1935.
—— *Time, Forward!* Trans. by Charles Malamuth. New York, Farrar & Rinehart, 1933.
KAVERIN, VENIAMIN. *The Larger View.* Trans. by E. Leda Swan. New York, C. Stackpole, 1938.
—— *Two Captains.* Trans. by E. Leda Swan. New York, Modern Age Books, 1942.

MODERN RUSSIAN LITERATURE IN ENGLISH

KAZIN, VASILI. *The Heavenly Factory.* (In Patrick, p. 214)
―――― *Poems.* (In Deutsch, pp. 224–25)
KIRSHON, VLADIMIR. *Bread.* (In Lyons, pp. 225–310)
――――, and A. USPENSKI. *Red Rust.* Adapted by Virginia and Frank Vernon. New York, Brentano's, 1930.
KLYUYEV, NIKOLAI. *Poems.* (In Deutsch, pp. 162–63)
―――― *Poems.* (In Patrick, pp. 221–24)
KOROLENKO, VLADIMIR. *The Blind Musician.* Trans. by William Westall and Sergius Stepniak. New York, J. W. Lovell, 1890.
―――― *In a Strange Land.* Trans. by Gregory Zilboorg. New York, B. G. Richards, 1925.
―――― *Makar's Dream.* Trans. by Marian Fell. New York, Duffield, 1916.
KROPOTKIN, PETER. *Memoirs of a Revolutionist.* Boston, Houghton Mifflin, 1930.
KUPRIN, ALEXANDER. *The Bracelet of Garnets.* Trans. by Leo Pasvolsky. New York, Scribner's, 1917.
―――― *The Duel.* New York, Macmillan, 1916.
―――― *Gambrinus.* Trans. by Bernard Guilbert Guerncy. New York, Adelphi, 1925.
―――― *The River of Life.* Trans. by S. Koteliansky and J. M. Murry. Boston, J. W. Luce, 1916.
―――― *Sasha.* Trans. by Douglas Ashby. Philadelphia, D. McKay, 1928.
―――― *A Slav Soul.* Trans. by Rosa Graham. New York, G. P. Putnam's, 1916.
―――― *Sulamith.* Trans. by Bernard Guilbert Guerney. New York, N. L. Brown, 1923.

MODERN RUSSIAN LITERATURE IN ENGLISH

LANDAU, M. A. *The Devil's Bridge.* New York, A. Knopf, 1928.
—— *The Key.* London, George G. Harap, 1931.
—— *The Ninth Thermidor.* New York, A. Knopf, 1928.
—— *Saint Helena, Little Island.* New York, A. Knopf, 1924.
LEONOV, LEONID. *Skutarevsky.* Trans. by Alec Brown. New York, Harcourt, Brace, 1936.
—— *Sot.* Trans. by Ivor Montagu and Sergei Nalbandov. New York, G. P. Putnam's, 1931.
—— *Soviet River.* Trans. by Ivor Montagu and Sergei Nalbandov. New York, Dial Press, 1932.
—— *The Thief.* Trans. by Hubert Butler. New York, Dial Press, 1931.
LIBEDINSKI, YURI. *A Week.* Trans. by Arthur Ransome. New York, B. W. Huebsch, 1923.
LOTARYOV, IGOR. *Poems.* (In Deutsch, pp. 159–61)
LUNACHARSKI, ANATOLI. *Three Plays.* Trans. by L. A. Magnus and K. Walter. New York, E. P. Dutton, 1923.
MANDELSTAM, O. E. *The Twilight of Freedom.* (In Coxwell, p. 252)
MAYAKOVSKI, V. V. *Lines to a Judge.* (In Coxwell, pp. 250–51)
—— *Mystery-Bouffe.* Trans. by G. R. Noyes and A. Kaun. (In Noyes, pp. 801–81)
—— *Poems.* (In Reavey, pp. 360–67)
—— *Poems.* (In *The American Quarterly on the Soviet Union;* July, 1940; pp. 60–96)
MEREZHKOVSKI, DMITRI. *The Birth of the Gods.* Trans. by

MODERN RUSSIAN LITERATURE IN ENGLISH Natalie A. Duddington. New York, E. P. Dutton, 1926.

MEREZHKOVSKI, DMITRI. *Jesus Manifest.* Trans. by Edward Gellibrand. New York, Scribner's, 1936.
—— *Jesus the Unknown.* Trans. by E. N. Matheson. New York, Scribner's, 1934.
—— *Julian the Apostate.* Trans. by Bernard Guilbert Guerney. New York, Modern Library, 1929.
—— *The Life of Napoleon.* Trans. by Catherine Zveginsova.
—— *Peter and Alexis.* Trans. by Bernard Guilbert Guerney. New York, Modern Library, 1937.
—— *Poems.* (In Deutsch, pp. 85-7)
—— *The Romance of Leonardo da Vinci.* Trans. by Bernard Guilbert Guerney. New York, Modern Library, 1928.
—— *Tolstoi as Man and Artist.* New York, G. P. Putnam's, 1902.

NABOKOV, V. V. *Despair.* London, John Long, 1937.
—— *Laughter in the Dark.* Indianapolis, Bobbs-Merrill, 1938.

NADSON, S. Y. *Poems.* (In Coxwell, pp. 192-93)

NOVIKOV-PRIBOI, ALEKSEI. *Tsushima.* Trans. by Eden and Cedar Paul. New York, A. Knopf, 1937.

OBRADOVICH, SERGEI. *Poems.* (In Patrick, pp. 237-40)

OLESHA, YURI. *The Cherry Stone.* (In Reavey, pp. 171-80)
—— *The Cherry Stone.* (In Montagu, pp. 1-10)

ORESHIN, P. V. *Poems.* (In Patrick, pp. 241-44)

OSORGIN, M. A., *pseud.* See Ilyin, M. A.

MODERN RUSSIAN LITERATURE IN ENGLISH

OSTROVSKI, NIKOLAI. *Born of the Storm.* Trans. by Louise Luke Hiler. New York, Critics' Group Press, 1939.

PANFEROV, FYODOR. *And Then the Harvest.* Trans. by Stephen Garry. London, G. P. Putnam's, 1939.

—— *Brusski.* Trans. by Z. Mitrov and J. Tabrisky. New York, International Publishers, 1930.

PASTERNAK, BORIS. *Childhood.* Trans. by Robert Payne. Singapore, Straits Times Press, 1941.

—— *Poems.* (In Reavey, pp. 377–388)

—— *Resting Oars.* (In Coxwell, p. 253)

PAVLENKO, PETER. *Red Planes Fly East.* Trans. by Stephen Garry. London, G. Routledge, 1938.

PETROV, YEVGENI, *joint author.* See Ilf, Ilya, and Yevgeni Petrov.

PILNYAK, BORIS, *pseud.* See Vogau, Boris.

POGODIN, NIKOLAI. *Tempo.* (In Lyons, pp. 155–224)

POPOV, ALEXANDER. *The Iron Flood.* New York, International Publishers, 1935.

PRIDVOROV, YEFIM. *Poems.* (In Deutsch, pp. 214–16)

PRISHVIN, MIKHAIL. *Jen Sheng: The Root of Life.* Trans. by George Walton and Philip Gibbons. New York, G. P. Putnam's, 1936.

ROMANOV, PANTELEIMON. *The New Commandment.* Trans. by Valentine Snow. New York, Scribner's, 1933.

—— *On the Volga.* Trans. by Ann Gretton. New York, Scribner's, 1934.

—— *Three Pairs of Silk Stockings.* Trans. by Leonide Zarine. New York, Scribner's, 1931.

—— *Without Cherry Blossom.* Trans. by Leonide Zarine. New York, Scribner's, 1932.

SEIFULLINA, LYDIA. *The Lawbreakers.* (In Reavey, pp. 129–36)
—— *The Lawbreakers.* (In Friedland, pp. 61–113)
SELVINSKI, ILYA. *The Golden Melody.* (In Reavey, pp. 370–71)
SERAFIMOVICH, A., *pseud.* See Popov, Alexander.
SERGEYEV-TSENSKI, SERGEI. *Transfiguration.* Trans. by Marie Budberg. New York, R. M. McBride, 1926.
SEVERYANIN, IGOR, *pseud.* See Lotaryov, Igor.
SHESTOV, LEO. *In Job's Balances.* Trans. by Camilla Coventry and C. A. Macartney. London, J. M. Dent, 1932.
SHOLOKHOV, MIKHAIL. *And Quiet Flows the Don.* Trans. by Stephen Garry. New York, A. Knopf, 1934.
—— *The Don Flows Home to the Sea.* Trans. by Stephen Garry. New York, A. Knopf. 1941.
—— *The Silent Don:* Vol. I, *And Quiet Flows the Don;* Vol. II, *The Don Flows Home to the Sea.* Trans. by Stephen Garry. New York, A. Knopf, 1942.
—— *Virgin Soil Upturned.* Trans. by Stephen Garry. London, G. P. Putnam's, 1935.
SIRIN, V. V., *pseud.* See Nabokov, V. V.
SMIDOWICZ, V. V. *The Deadlock.* Trans. by Nina Wissotzky and Camilla Coventry. New York, Century, 1928.
—— *The Sisters.* Trans. by Juliet Soskice. London, Hutchinson & Co., 1934.
SOLOGUB, FYODOR, *pseud.* See Teternikov, F. K.
SOLOVYOV, VLADIMIR. *War and Christianity.* New York, G. P. Putnam's, 1915.
TETERNIKOV, F. K. *The Little Demon.* Trans. by John

Cournos and Richard Aldington. New York, A. Knopf, 1916.
TETERNIKOV, F. K. *Poems.* (In Deutsch, pp. 88–92)
TIKHONOV, NIKOLAI. *Poems.* (In Reavey, pp. 368–69)
—— *Yorgyi.* (In Reavey, pp. 204–16)
TOLSTOI, ALEKSEI. *Bread.* Trans. by Stephen Garry. London, V. Gollancz, 1938.
—— *Darkness and Dawn.* Trans. by Edith Bone and Emile Burns. New York, Longmans, Green, 1936.
—— *Peter the Great.* Trans. by Edith Bone and Emile Burns. London, V. Gollancz, 1936.
—— *The Road to Calvary.* Trans. by R. S. Townsend. New York, Boni and Liveright, 1923.
TRETYAKOV, SERGEI. *A Chinese Testament.* New York, Simon and Schuster, 1934.
—— *Roar China!* Trans. by F. Polianovska and Barbara Nixon. London, M. Lawrence, 1931.
TYNYANOV, YURI. *Death and Diplomacy in Persia.* London, Boriswood, 1938.
—— *Second Lieutenant Also.* (In Montagu, *Soviet Short Stories,* pp. 41–69)
USHAKOV, NIKOLAI. *Karabash.* (In Reavey, pp. 272–73)
USPENSKI, ANDREI, *joint author.* See Kirshon, Vladimir.
VERESAYEV, V. V., *pseud.* See Smidowicz, V. V.
VOGAU, BORIS. *Ivan Moscow.* Trans. by A. Schwartzman. Boston, Christopher Publishing House, 1935.
—— *The Law of the Wolf.* (In Robbins, pp. 173–223)
—— *Leather Jackets.* (In Friedland, pp. 56–60)
—— *The Naked Year.* Trans. by Alec Brown. New York, Payson & Clarke, 1928.

MODERN RUSSIAN LITERATURE IN ENGLISH

VOGAU, BORIS. *Tales of the Wilderness.* Trans. by F. O'Dempsey. New York, A. Knopf, 1925.
────── *The Volga Falls to the Caspian Sea.* Trans. by Charles Malamuth. New York, Cosmopolitan Book Corp., 1931.
VOLOSHIN, MAXIMILIAN. *Poems.* (In Deutsch, pp. 130–33)
YESENIN, SERGEI. *Poems.* (In Deutsch, pp. 166–70, 191)
────── *Poems.* (In Patrick, pp. 182–92)
ZAITSEV, B. K. *Anna.* New York, Holt, 1937.
ZAMYATIN, EVGENI. *We.* Trans. by Gregory Zilboorg. New York, E. P. Dutton, 1924.
ZOSHCHENKO, MIKHAIL. *Dawn of the New Day.* (In Montagu, pp. 83–149)
────── *Russia Laughs.* Trans. by Helena Clayton. Boston, Lothrop, Lee and Shepard, 1935.
────── *The Woman Who Could Not Read.* Trans. by E. Fen. London, Methuen & Co., 1940.
────── *The Wonderful Dog.* Trans. by E. Fen. London, Methuen & Co., 1942.

SELECTED BIBLIOGRAPHY OF LITERARY HISTORY AND CRITICISM IN ENGLISH

BARING, MAURICE. *An Outline of Russian Literature.* New York, Holt, 1915.
DANA, H. W. L. *Handbook on Soviet Drama.* New York, American Russian Institute, 1938.
FREEMAN, J., J. KUNITZ, and L. LOZOWICK. *Voices of Octo-*

ber: *Art and Literature in Soviet Russia.* New York, Vanguard Press, 1930.

LAUGHLIN, JAMES, editor. *New Directions in Prose and Poetry, 1941.* Norfolk, Conn., New Directions, 1941.

LAVRIN, JANKO. *An Introduction to the Russian Novel.* London, Methuen & Co., 1942.

LONDON, KURT. *The Seven Soviet Arts.* New Haven, Conn., Yale University Press, 1938.

MARKOV, P. A. *The Soviet Theatre.* London, V. Gollancz, 1934.

MILIUKOV, PAUL. *Outlines of Russian Culture, Part II: Literature;* trans. by Valentine Ughet and Eleanor Davis and edited by Michael Karpovich. Philadelphia, University of Pennsylvania Press, 1942.

MIRSKY, D. S. *Contemporary Russian Literature: 1881–1925.* London, G. Routledge, 1926.

Problems of Soviet Literature. Reports and Speeches at the First Soviet Writers' Congress. Moscow, Cooperative Publishing Society of Foreign Workers in the U.S.S.R., 1935.

STRUVE, GLEB. *Soviet Russian Literature.* London, G. Routledge, 1935.

International Literature, passim.

Slavonic and East European Review, passim.

Index

Afinogenov, A. N., 66, 67-68
Akhmatova, Anna, 36
Aldanov, M. A., 56-57
Alexander II, 4, 5
Alexander III, 5
Andreyev, Leonid, 16, 20-21, 22, 23, 39
Annenski, I. F., 29
Apukhtin, A. N., 13
Artsybashev, M. P., 21-22
Aseyev, Nikolai, 62
Averbakh, L., 49

Babel, Isaak, 42, 43, 66
Bagritski, Eduard, 62
Balmont, K. D., 28, 39
Baudelaire, Charles, 27
Bedny, Demyan, 60
Beethoven, Ludwig van, 56
Belinski, V. G., 4, 73
Belotserkovski, Bill, V. N., see Bill-Belotserkovski, V. N.
Bely, Andrei, 31-32, 34, 39, 42, 48
Benois, A., 23
Bezymenski, A. I., 59, 61, 62
Bill-Belotserkovski, V. N., 66
Blake, William, 13
Blok, A. A., 33-35, 36, 39
Bryusov, Valeri, 27-28, 30, 34, 39
Budantsev, Sergei, 70
Bugayev, Boris, see Bely, Andrei

Bulgakov, Mikhail, 47, 53-54, 66
Bunin, I. A., 19-20, 39

Catherine II, 56
Chapygin, Aleksei, 71-72
Chekhov, Anton Pavlovich, 9-11, 15, 16, 18, 19, 21, 44, 45
Chernyshevski, N. G., 73
Chirikov, E. N., 18

Dante Alighieri, 61
Diaghilev, Sergei, 23
Doronin, Ivan, 61
Dos Passos, John, 51
Dostoyevsky, Fyodor, 3, 4, 5, 12, 24, 25, 26, 27, 30, 31, 32, 44, 45
Duncan, Isadora, 38

Ehrenburg, Ilya, 53
Erdman, N., 66
Ertel, A. I., 8

Fadeyev, Alexander, 42, 46-47
Fedin, K., 40, 42, 44-45, 66
Fet, A. A., 12
Flekser, A. L., see Volynski
Furmanov, Dmitri, 42, 43

Garshin, V. M., 7
Gastev, A. K., 60
Gerasimov, M. P., 60

91

INDEX

Gladkov, F. V., 51, 66
Gogol, N., 9, 31
Golodny, Mikhail, 61
Goncharov, A. I., 4, 12
Gorky, Maxim, 15-17, 18, 19, 20, 21, 23, 40, 49
Gorodetski, Sergei, 36
Griboyedov, A. S., 72
Gumilyov, N. S., 36

Herzen, A. I., 8, 73
Hippius, Zinaida, 23-24, 29, 39
Hitler, Adolf, 53
Hood, Thomas, 13

Ilf, Ilya, 54
Ilyin, M. A., see Osorgin, M. A.
Ivanov, Vsevolod, 40, 42, 43, 46, 66, 67
Ivanov, Vyacheslav, 29-30

Joyce, James, 32

Katayev, V., 41, 51, 54, 66
Kaverin, Veniamin, 40, 70
Kazin, Vasili, 61
Khlebnikov, Velemir, 36
Khodasevich, V. F., 33
Kipling, Rudyard, 19
Kirshon, Vladimir, 67
Klyuyev, N. A., 60
Korolenko, V. G., 8-9, 16
Kropotkin, Peter, 8
Küchelbecker, W., 72
Kuprin, A. I., 18-19, 39

Landau, M. A., see Aldanov, M. A.
Lelevich, G., 63
Lenin, V. I., 14, 40, 58, 60, 71

Leonov, Leonid, 41, 45-46, 50, 66
Lermontov, Mikhail, 35
Leskov, N. S., 4
Libedinski, Yuri, 55
London, Jack, 19
Lunacharski, A. V., 40, 66

Malashkin, Sergei, 70
Mallarmé, Stéphane, 27
Mandelstam, O. E., 36
Marinetti, P., 37
Marx, Karl, 14
Mayakovski, V. V., 36-37, 38, 40, 58-59, 60, 61, 62, 67
Merezhkovski, D. S., 23-25, 27, 39
Minski, 24, 39

Nabokov, V. V., 57
Nadson, Semyon, 12-13
Nekrasov, N. A., 12, 58
Neverov, Alexander, 47, 66
Nicholas I, 5
Nietzsche, Friedrich, 26
Novikov-Priboi, A., 72

Obradovich, Sergei, 63
Olesha, Yuri, 66, 67, 70
Oreshin, P. V., 60
Osorgin, M. A., 55-56
Ostrovski, Nikolai, 70

Panferov, F., 52
Pasternak, Boris, 62-63
Paul I, 56
Pavlenko, P., 72
Peshkov, A. M., see Gorky, Maxim
Petrov, Evgeni, 54
Petrov, S. G., see Skitalets
Pilnyak, Boris, 41, 42-43, 50

INDEX

Poe, Edgar Allan, 27
Pogodin, N. F., 67
Popov, A. S., *see* Serafimovich, A. S.
Priboi, Novikov, A., *see* Novikov-Priboi, A.
Pridvorov, Yefim, *see* Bedny, Demyan
Prishvin, Mikhail, 48
Pushkin, A. S., 12, 33, 58, 72

Razin, Stenka, 72
Remizov, A. M., 32, 39, 42, 48
Robespierre, I. M. de, 56
Rodov, Semyon, 63
Romanov, Panteleimon, 55
Romashov, B. S., 66
Rozanov, V. V., 25-26, 27

Schwarzmann, L. I., *see* Shestov, Leo
Seifullina, Lydia, 47, 66
Selvinski, Ilya, 62
Serafimovich, A. S., 18, 39
Sergeyev-Tsenski, S. N., 39, 55, 71
Severyanin, Igor, 36, 39
Shestov, Leo, 26, 27
Shmelyov, Ivan, 18, 39
Sholokhov, Mikhail, 47, 52
Sirin, V. V., *see* Nabokov, V. V.
Skitalets, 18
Slonimski, Mikhail, 47
Smidowicz, V. V., *see* Veresayev, V. V.
Sologub, Fyodor, 30-31
Solovyov, V. S., 13, 31, 33
Stalin, Joseph, 49, 71
Steiner, Rudolf, 31

Suvorov, A. V., 56
Svetlov, Mikhail, 61

Teternikov, F. K., *see* Sologub
Tikhonov, Nikolai, 40, 63
Tolstoy, A. N., 39, 46, 66, 71
Tolstoy, Leo, 3, 4, 5, 7, 8, 12, 16, 19, 20, 21, 24, 44, 46, 52, 68, 73
Trotsky, Leon, 40, 41, 60
Trenev, K. A., 66, 67
Tretyakov, S. M., 66, 67
Tsenski, Sergeyev, *see* Sergeyev-Tsenski
Tsvetayeva, Marina, 39
Turgenev, I. S., 3, 4, 5, 7, 9, 12, 19, 56
Tynyanov, Yuri, 72
Tyutchev, F. I., 12

Ushakov, Nikolai, 61

Veresayev, V. V., 18, 39
Vesyoly, Artyom, 48
Vilenkin, N. M., *see* Minski
Vishnevski, V. V., 67
Vogau, B. A., *see* Pilnyak, Boris
Volynski, 24
Voronski, A., 40

Yesenin, Sergei, 38-39

Zaitsev, B. K., 56
Zamyatin, E. I., 40, 53
Zelinski, Kornely, 62
Zharov, Alexander, 61
Zilberg, *see* Kaverin, V.
Zoshchenko, M., 40, 54